He Set His Face *to* Jerusalem

He Set His Face *to* Jerusalem

A Lenten Study for Adults

RICHARD B. WILKE

Abingdon Press
Nashville

Library of Congress Cataloging-in-Publication Data

CIP data has been requested.

13 14 15 16 17 18 19 20 21 22—10 9 8 7 6 5 4 3 2 1
MANUFACTURED IN THE UNITED STATES OF AMERICA

Contents

Introduction

Jesus Set His Face Toward Jerusalem

J esus set his face toward Jerusalem and in so doing, he offered us God's life, power, and salvation. As followers of Jesus, we are called to reflect on and pray about where we set our faces day by day. Where do we set our faces in our relationships with God and with our neighbor? Where do we set our faces with our ethical choices? Where do we set our faces when we see those who are poor and oppressed? These are examples of questions we ask ourselves and one another as we look at Jesus' decisions during the season of Lent.

In the Christian church, Lent is a season of forty days of repentance and fasting to help people prepare for Easter. Sundays are not counted because they are considered to be "mini-celebrations" of the Resurrection. The season begins with Ash Wednesday and lasts through the Saturday before Easter. On Ash Wednesday, many of us receive dust and ashes on our foreheads. We remember that we will return to dust and ashes, we repent, and we offer gratitude that, through Jesus' resurrection, God offers us life and salvation. The origins of the word *Lent* include a cluster of Old English and Germanic words that point to the lengthening days of spring. Longer days means spring-time, and spring means newness of life—the dead days of winter are gone. Resurrection is coming!

In the Bible, the number *forty* is highly symbolic for prayer, sacrifice, sober thought, and preparation. Remember, in the story of Noah and the ark, the rain fell for forty days and forty nights (Genesis 7:12). Moses and the people of Israel were forty years in the wilderness—often with only manna from heaven to eat as they journeyed toward the Promised Land (Deuteronomy 8:3; 29:5-6). Jesus began his ministry by going into the wilderness for forty days, praying hard, fasting to the point of death, preparing for his ministry (Matthew 4:1-11).

During this season of Lent, we set aside time to read the Scriptures, pray alone and in fellowship, study, and discuss our Lord's saving ministry. In this particular Lenten study, we will focus on the closing days of our Lord's words and work. We will begin when Jesus closed his Galilean work; went on to a mountainside with Peter, James, and John; prayed almost all night; then "set his face to Jerusalem." We will carefully ponder that critical decision—and decide how we might make life-determining decisions about where we set our faces. We will observe Jesus' healings and his teachings along the way. We will be overwhelmed to visualize the huge Roman army entering Jerusalem from the west on Passover Sunday (Palm Sunday), the same day Jesus rode into the city on a little donkey. We will meditate on "The Last Supper"—thinking about times we have a "last supper" with relatives and friends. And we will experience the origin of Holy Communion. Then we will go into the garden of Gethsemane for a night of prayer. Does Jesus really want to go through with the unbelievable pain and suffering that lay ahead? We will finish our study meditating on our Lord's final words from the cross—and we will be spiritually ready for Resurrection, for a glorious, victorious Easter morning!

Richard B. Wilke
Bishop-in-Residence
Southwestern College
Winfield, Kansas

He Set His Face

Scripture: Read Luke 9:28-62.

Have you ever "set your face" to do something? Jesus did! He was in Galilee, among many small farming villages where thousands gladly listened to him. He performed healings. He reached out to marginalized people, like lepers standing by the wayside. He even blessed and healed some hated Samaritans. A few religious lawyers, Pharisees, and rabbis criticized him; but in Galilee, he was in fairly safe territory.

Jerusalem was the center of political and religious power. Jesus knew full well that if he went to Jerusalem, he would challenge the muscle of the Roman Empire. He would offend those among the priests and Pharisees who had sold out to the Romans in order to obtain and keep their Temple positions. Jesus not only knew what he faced in terms of conflict, he knew that he would be arrested, put on trial, convicted of treason, beaten, crucified, and killed by the authorities. He was completely aware of the certain tragic consequences of his choice, yet he made a clear decision. As the New Revised Standard Version translates it, Jesus "set his face to go to Jerusalem" (verse 51).

Jesus Decides

Decisions often emerge from strange and unlikely places. For Jesus, the decision emerged on a lonely mountain in the experience of the Transfiguration. He took Peter, John, and James, and went up on a mountain to pray. As he was praying, the appearance of his face changed and his clothes flashed white like lightning. Two men, Moses and Elijah, were talking with him. They were clothed with heavenly splendor and spoke about Jesus' departure, which he would achieve in Jerusalem. Peter and those with him were almost overcome by sleep, but they managed to stay awake and saw his glory as well as the two men with him.

As the two men were about to leave Jesus, Peter said to him, "Master, it's good that we're here. We should construct three shrines: one for you, one for Moses, and one for Elijah"—but he didn't know what he was saying. Peter was still speaking when a cloud overshadowed them. As they entered the cloud, they were overcome with awe.

They heard a voice that said, "This is my Son, my chosen one. Listen to him!" (Luke 9:28-35; see also Mark 9:2-7; Matthew 17:1-5).

In Matthew's Gospel, Jesus came and touched them. " 'Get up,' he said. 'Don't be afraid' " (Matthew 17:7). Peter wanted to stay, but Jesus had made his decision;

they came down from the mountain, and they were met by a large crowd (Luke 9:37). In the midst of conflict and in spite of impending danger, Jesus made a life-determining decision. He "set his face to go to Jerusalem" (9:51, NRSV).

For us, a life-determining decision might come from a job we worked at as a kid, from a chance remark made by a friend or a teacher, from a youth camp experience, or from a night in prayer. A high school coach sees a twelve-year-old kid running fast and says, "Why don't you learn to play soccer?" Ten years later that "kid" is winning a soccer championship and graduating from the state university. A husband commits adultery; his wife files for divorce; he gets on his knees in prayer and makes a decision to ask her for forgiveness. They enter marriage counseling, go to church, hold hands, and save their marriage. A pastor casually speaks to a high school student, "Have you ever thought about going into the ministry?" He or she never has before but now does and eight or ten years later, that person is pastoring a church and preaching the gospel.

Such life-determining decisions occur with other key figures in the Bible. Do you remember Abram, who became Abraham? He and his wife Sarai, who was unable to have children, had settled safely in Haran with other family members and many possessions. Then, "the LORD said to Abram, 'Leave your land, your family, and your father's household for the land that I will show you. I will make of you a great nation and will bless you'" (Genesis 12:1-2). So

"Abram left just as the LORD told him, and Lot went with him. Now Abram was 75 years old when he left Haran...and they set out for the land of Canaan" (Genesis 12:4-5).

After a long drought and a time of famine, Abram and Sarai fled to Egypt to survive, to get food for themselves and their servants (Genesis 12:10). Afraid of Pharaoh's power, and knowing that Sarai was beautiful, Abram said she was his sister. Pharaoh at first planned to take Sarai as another of his wives, but he found out the truth and sent Abram and Sarai packing (Genesis 12:11-20). Then, returning to Canaan, Abram's servants quarreled with his nephew Lot's servants. In a gracious moment, Abraham gave Lot his choice of land; Lot took the sumptuous farmland, and Abram got the dry pastures (Genesis 13:1-12). Later Abram showed his family loyalty by saving Lot in warfare (Genesis 14:1-16). After a battle with some enemy kings who had stolen Lot's possessions, Abram won the fight, restored the herds to Lot, gave a tenth of the flock to the priest Melchizedek, and refused to "take even a thread or a sandal strap" for himself (Genesis 14:17-23).

Then the Lord's word came to Abram in a vision, "Don't be afraid, Abram....Your reward will be very great." But Abram said, "LORD God, what can you possibly give me, since I still have no children?" (Genesis 15:1-2). Then God said, "'Look up at the sky and count the stars if you think you can count them.' He continued, 'This is how many children you will have'" (Genesis 15:5).

So Abram and Sarai obeyed God, became Abraham and Sarah, became parents, and became the father and mother of the entire Hebrew people—millions today—and the father of Jewish, Christian, and Muslim people around the world. All of this because Abram was willing to make a prayerful, obedient decision to leave his traditional supportive family and friends in Haran and set out to unknown territories of Canaan.

Do you remember Moses? Born a Hebrew in Egypt, raised by Pharaoh's daughter, a killer of an Egyptian soldier who murdered a Hebrew slave, a runaway sheep herder in the Sinai desert—now, married, working for his father-in-law, and middle-aged, Moses goes to a bush that is strangely on fire. Then Moses said to himself, "Let me check out this amazing sight and find out why the bush isn't burning up" (Exodus 3:3). Big Deal! But it is decision time.

Moses hid his face but God spoke: "'I've clearly seen my people oppressed in Egypt. . . . I know about their pain. . . . So get going. I'm sending you to Pharaoh to bring my people, the Israelites, out of Egypt.' But Moses said to God, 'Who am I to go to Pharaoh and to bring the Israelites out of Egypt?' God said, 'I'll be with you'" (Exodus 3:7, 10-12). Moses objected again, "They are going to ask me, 'What's this God's name?' What am I supposed to say to them?" God responded, "I Am Who I Am. So say to the Israelites, 'I Am has sent me to you'" (Exodus 3:13-14). Once again Moses objects: "My Lord, I've never been able to speak well. . . . I have a slow mouth and a thick tongue. . . . Please, my Lord, just send someone else" (Exodus 4:10, 13).

"Then the LORD got angry at Moses and said, 'What about your brother, Aaron the Levite? I know he can speak very well....I'll help both of you speak, and I'll teach both of you what to do'" (Exodus 4:14-15).

That short little episode in the Sinai, that brief conversation with God at the burning bush, that life-determining decision to go back to Egypt—think of the results! The escape of the Hebrews from Egypt, the forty years in the wilderness, the Ten Commandments, the establishment of priests and elders, the preparation for Joshua to lead the people into the Promised Land, ultimately the building of the Temple in Jerusalem, all because of a prayer discussion with God near a burning bush!

Or imagine the life changes when the Twelve called together the community of faith to resolve a conflict between Hellenists (Jews and Jewish Christians who spoke Greek) and Hebrews (Jews and Jewish Christians who spoke Aramaic as well as Greek) about the distribution of food. The solution was to separate the ministries and designate leadership. The disciples chose seven men to lead the ministry of food distribution while the Twelve continued their ministry of word and prayer. Among the seven were Stephen and Philip (Acts 6:1-7).

Their decision had far-reaching ramifications. Soon Stephen, full of the Holy Spirit, would boldly testify in Jerusalem, causing him to be stoned to death (Acts 6:8–7:60). Note that a Pharisee, whose Hebrew name was Saul, held the coats of those who threw the rocks. But Saul, who heard the testimony of Stephen, experienced a dramatic conversion as he traveled to Damascus (Acts 9:1-9). Just think of the thousands of Gentiles and Jews converted by Saul, also known by his Greco-Roman name, Paul. And Philip preached in Samaria, on the road from Jerusalem to Gaza, in Azotus, and in Caesarea (Acts 8). On the road from Jerusalem to Gaza, he encountered and witnessed to an Ethiopian eunuch, a court official for the Ethiopian queen. He was returning from worship in Jerusalem (Acts 8:27). As a result of hearing Philip's testimony of good news about Jesus, the eunuch asked to be baptized. After his baptism, tradition has it that he went back to Ethiopia and founded the Ethiopian church.

Jesus went to the mountain for a night of prayer—the disciples wanted to celebrate a spiritual encounter. But Jesus had a different, life-determining choice in mind that would lead him to challenge civil and religious leaders in Jerusalem and to give his life as a sacrifice of love for the sins of the whole world. A world-changing decision was made. After a night of prayer with the three apostles and a heavenly vision, Jesus is prepared for the worst: "Take these words to heart: The Human One [or the Son of Man] is about to be delivered into human hands" (Luke 9:44).

Obstacles and Opportunities

Immediately, obstacles appeared even before Jesus got underway. The very next day, as they came down from the mountain of prayer, a father cried out, "Teacher, I beg you to take a look at my son, my only child. Look, a spirit seizes him and, without any warning, he screams. It shakes him and causes him to foam at the mouth.... I begged your disciples to throw it out, but they couldn't" (Luke 9:38-40). "Jesus spoke harshly to the unclean spirit, healed the child, and gave him back to his father" (Luke 9:42b-43). Jesus was ready to travel south, but he could not deny the weeping father or the violently sick son. Sometimes as we get ready for a journey, an emergency strikes, or some unfinished task is still on the table. We must do what we have to do, even as we travel. Jesus the Healer acted quickly.

Then they started walking. But opposition slapped at Jesus from every direction, and Jesus used opposition as an opportunity to teach. First, the disciples started arguing about who would be the greatest. Jesus, frustrated, must have been shaking his head. He picked up a little child and said, "Whoever welcomes this child in my name welcomes me.... Whoever is least among you all is the greatest" (Luke 9:48). The mother of James and John came to Jesus, bowed down, and asked a favor. " 'What do you want?' he asked. She responded, 'Say that these two sons of mine will sit, one on your right hand and one on your left, in your kingdom' " (Matthew 20:21). After the other disciples became angry and fussed at them, Jesus said, "Whoever wants to be great among you will be your servant. Whoever wants to be first among you will be your slave" (Matthew 20:26-27).

In the midst of obstacles and opportunities, it was time to travel. The New Revised Standard Version of the Bible says that Jesus "set his face to go to Jerusalem," and the Common English Bible says that he "determined to go to Jerusalem" (Luke 9:51). Setting one's face is a powerful visual image of deep determination. Sometimes a life-determining decision may be easier than following through and staying committed to the decision.

As he entered a Samaritan village, the people were angry. They "refused to welcome him because he was determined to go to Jerusalem" (Luke 9:53). Why? For centuries, Jews and Samaritans had demonstrated animosity toward one another. They worshiped separately. The Samaritan woman who had conversation with Jesus at the well had said, "Our ancestors worshipped on this mountain, but you and your people say that it is necessary to worship in Jerusalem" (John 4:20). The Samaritans remembered Jesus' reply: "The time is coming when you and your people will worship the Father neither on this mountain nor in Jerusalem.... The time is coming—and is here!—when true worshippers will worship in spirit and in truth" (John 4:21, 23). Anger at the Samaritans welled up in the disciples; they wanted to call down fire from heaven to consume the villagers (Luke 9:54). But Jesus rebuked the disciples and moved on, neither angry nor sidetracked.

The next delay came from prospective followers. One man volunteered to join them but wanted to wait awhile, "First let me go and bury my father" (Luke 9:59). Jesus refused him. "Let the dead bury their own dead," he said. Then another claimed he wanted to go home and say goodbye to his family and household. Jesus is "on the road again" and rebukes the man: "No one who puts a hand on the plow and looks back is fit for God's kingdom" (Luke 9:62). There comes a moment when it is "time to fish or cut bait." Jesus had "set his face" and called his followers to do the same.

The greatest opposition came from the disciples when they realized Jesus was dead serious and was headed for confrontation with the authorities where he would encounter trouble, torture, and even death. In Matthew's Gospel, Jesus began to tell his disciples that "he had to go to Jerusalem and suffer many things from the elders, chief priests, and legal experts, and that he had to be killed and raised on the third day." But Peter took hold of Jesus, scolded him, and tried to change him: "God forbid, Lord! This won't happen to you." But Jesus cried out, "Get behind me, Satan. You are a stone that could make me stumble, for you are not thinking God's thoughts but human thoughts" (Matthew 16:21-23). Jesus refused to allow Peter to distract or deter him.

Where Do We Set Our Faces?

This story of mine may sound trivial, but a prayerful moment and a little decision changed my life. In college, my girlfriend and I were winding up a happy "date." We sat in the back seat of a friend's car (I had no wheels). We had been going to movies, dancing 'til midnight, yelling together at the SMU football games for several months. Now at the close of this particular evening, we were kissing and hugging and kissing some more as young folks sometimes do. Suddenly, Julia broke it off and whispered softly, "Dick, do you love me?" Those simple words were like a bolt of lightning. I leaned back, closed my eyes, and thought, as if I were on the mountain in prayer, as if I were in the very presence of God. I thought. *My goodness, she's asking if I am dead serious. She's wanting a lifetime commitment. She's not playing games: she wants a decision— good Lord, a wedding!*

I sat in quiet darkness for a few moments. Then, suddenly something clicked within me. No equivocation. No waffling—a clean, clear decision. I was ready. I turned, looked into her beautiful blue-green eyes, and said softly, with full commitment, "Yes, I do love you!" The life-determining decision was made. Now, over sixty years later, I still love her. It was a wise moment of decision.

You and I need to make prayerful decisions. We need to be open to God, and when God speaks, we need to make thoughtful and obedient decisions. We need to sing:

Open my eyes, that I may see glimpses of truth thou
    hast for me;
  place in my hands the wonderful key that shall
    unclasp and set me free.
Silently now I wait for thee, ready, my God, thy will to
    see.
Open my eyes, illumine me, Spirit divine![1]

When I was about twelve years old and active in our junior high fellowship, we had a special evening youth service. The speaker was a college student from Wichita, a pre-seminary student, I suppose. About a dozen of us kids were in the large sanctuary, sort of listening. Suddenly, I perked up my ears when he mentioned stars. I had been studying stars in Boy Scouts. "The North Star" he said, "is faithful and true." A ship in the ocean might set sail by other stars and get lost. But sailors can determine their course by the North Star and that star will never, ever fail them. (I'm listening) Suddenly, our young "preacher" said, "Jesus is like the North Star—always true, always faithful. You can set the sail of your life, guided by Jesus, the North Star, and you will never get lost." Then he said, "If you want to make Jesus the North Star of your life, come and kneel here at the altar." I went forward, along with a handful of others, and I said, "Jesus, I want you to be the North Star of my life." I decided, I prayerfully decided. I set my face, and I have never changed my mind. I haven't always been true to him, but like the North Star, he has always been true to me.

Years later, The Methodist Church celebrated a huge youth conference in Cleveland, Ohio, with over ten thousand youth from all over the world. Along with a handful of other kids from our little town, I went, slept in a gym, and listened to great speakers like E. Stanley Jones. One great preacher, Dr. Richard Raines, said, "Here's how you know where God is calling you to serve. First, contemplate a horizontal line representing the needs of the world. [We were living in the destructive aftermath of World War II.] Children are sick—a need for doctors and nurses; people are hungry—a need for food; some folks are nearly naked—a need for clothing; some have never heard about the saving love of Jesus—a need for preachers." Then, said Raines, crossing that horizontal line, visualize a vertical line: "That's you, with your individual gifts and graces—uniquely you. Where the horizontal line (the needs of the world) crosses the vertical line (your unique abilities)—that is where God is calling you." My best friend, Paul, decided God wanted him to be a doctor. He served as a dermatologist his entire professional life. In high school, I was a debater, in school plays, and active in our church. I bowed my head in prayer and decided that God wanted me to be preacher.

But a problem arose. My grandpa, Mom's dad, was a pharmacist turned funeral director with an emergency ambulance. Dad, an accountant, kept the books at night for the funeral home. Grandpa had a heart attack at age fifty-two, died on the spot, and left a widow, debt, and young daughters. My dad went to embalming school and took over the funeral home. He carried the business through the Dust Bowl years in Kansas, the Depression, when folks couldn't pay for their funerals (one destitute farmer gave Dad an old mule to make a symbolic payment). Dad carried the business through the war years of the 1940's when we were short on workers. As a teenager I helped unpack caskets, set up the chapel, and carry cots for the ambulance or on death calls. Now in the

1950's, Dad wanted to turn the now-thriving business over to me when I graduated from college. When I told him that God wanted me to become a preacher, he was not happy. He told me I was making a mistake—that I could serve God by helping families in their grief. He told me that he had worked hard day and night to prepare the business for me. In his tough, non-emotional way, he clamped his jaw for two years, hoping I would change my mind. But he could not dissuade me; I believed that God wanted me to be a preacher. I held my course; I had "set my face" to what God wanted me to do. Dad finally accepted the decision.

Maybe you have a sense of God's call to "set your face" in a particular direction. Jesus' life-determining decision to "set his face to Jerusalem" gave and continues to give life to us. Where we set our faces may well determine whether we, too, can participate in the life-determining, life-giving work of God.

Questions for Reflection and Discussion

1. Read Luke 9:28-36, 51 and the section "Jesus Decides." How do you think this experience of the Transfiguration may have helped Jesus "set his face to go to Jerusalem"?

2. Read Luke 9:37-51 and the section "Obstacles and Opportunities." How does this Scripture speak to you about Jesus' relationship to God and to those around him?

3. Read Luke 9:52-62. How does this Scripture passage speak to you about being a follower of Jesus Christ? What challenges you or inspires you? Why?

4. In the section "Where Do We Set Our Faces?" the writer describes several life-determining decisions in his life. How do you respond to the image of Jesus as the North Star? What images would you use to describe Jesus? Why?

5. How do you respond to the story about the writer's father opposing his decision to be a preacher? Have you had a similar experience? How did it turn out?

6. Do you have a sense of God's call to "set your face" in a particular direction? Toward where do you think you need to set your face? What might be your first step on the journey?

Prayer

Dear Lord, help me to hear your voice, even now, and learn that you want me to do certain things, go certain places, help certain people. Help me to obey and to "set my face" to do your will. Thank you, Jesus. Amen.

Focus for the Week

Setting our faces often means making and following through with a life-determining decision. This week, reflect on your experiences with setting your face in a particular direction. Write your story. What was one of your life-determining decisions? How do you think God was with you in the decision? Have you kept "on course" or did you get sidetracked? Did some folks try to divert you, change your mind or your direction? Did your journey, even under God's guidance, lead you "to Jerusalem," to difficulties, trials, or suffering? How did you get through the journey?

1. "Open My Eyes, That I May See," words and music by Clara H. Scott.

On the Road Again

Scripture: Read Matthew 5:1–7:28.

J ust because Jesus made the irrevocable decision to go to Jerusalem to confront the Temple
authorities and face the powers of the Roman
Empire did not mean he stopped his ministry. All
four Gospels show that his entire ministry as he walked
along the way to Jerusalem demonstrated the heartbeat of
God's laws of justice, mercy, and love. Let's look at some
of the stories about healings, teachings, and feeding along
the way.

Healings

Because so much of Jesus' ministry involved healing,
some refer to Jesus as the Great Physician (see Luke
4:23; Matthew 9:12-13). In Chapter 1 we noted that, even
as Jesus, Peter, James, and John came down from the
mountain, a man brought his epileptic son to Jesus' feet
and our Lord healed him (Luke 9:37-43).

Jesus' healings continued—sometimes encountering opposition. Jesus went to a synagogue on the Sabbath to teach. A woman slipped in—a lady so severely crippled, so bent over, that she could not stand up straight. She had been disabled for over eighteen years (Luke 13:10-17)! Over the years, in an effort to honor God's laws, religious leaders had surrounded the third commandment, "Keep the Sabbath day and treat it as holy" (Deuteronomy 5:12), with scores of more specific rules and interpretations. Those who challenged Jesus' healing believed that he dishonored the Sabbath. But our Lord placed his hands on her and she straightened up at once and praised God (Luke 13:10-13). Jesus looked the angry religious leaders in the face and said, "Hypocrites! Don't each of you on the Sabbath untie your ox or donkey from its stall and lead it out to get a drink? Then isn't it necessary that this woman, a daughter of Abraham, bound by Satan for eighteen long years, be set free from her bondage on the Sabbath day?" (Luke 13:15-16). The opponents were silenced, and the crowd rejoiced.

Luke's Gospel also records that, even as Jesus was traveling southward, he performed additional miracle healings. "On the way to Jerusalem, Jesus traveled along the border between Samaria and Galilee. As he entered a village, ten men with skin diseases approached him. Keeping their distance from him, they raised their voices and said, 'Jesus, Master, show us mercy!'" (Luke 17:11-13). In those days, people who were infected with leprosy and other skin diseases were considered to be unclean.

Jesus took pity on them and told them to "go, show your-selves to the priests." It was written in Jewish law that priests could verify healings and allow men and women to return to society and to Temple worship. Without that priestly verification, skin-diseased people continued to be excluded from society. (See Leviticus 13.) The ten were healed even as they departed. But one man turned around, came back, fell on his face before Jesus, and thanked him. Jesus commented that nine of the men did not come back to say "thank you." Still, Jesus healed them, one of whom, the one who gave thanks, was a Samaritan! These powerful healings all occurred while our Lord was walking toward his death (Luke 17:11-19).

We have so many people sick and dying today—all around the world! If only Jesus, the Great Physician, were here! But wait a minute: Do you recall these words Jesus spoke before he was crucified? He told Philip, "I assure you that whoever believes in me will do the works that I do. They will do even greater works than these because I am going to the Father" (John 14:12). You and I can-not speak and cure a leper, nor can we say to a crippled woman, "Stand up straight." But look at what Christians have done in the name of Jesus! Think back across twenty centuries and recall monasteries all over Europe, caring for the sick and dying. John Wesley and the early Method-ists prayed for the sick and gave healing care. Now, with modern medicine, look at today's world. Visit St. Jude Children's Research Hospital in Memphis, Tennessee, or the Methodist Hospital system in Houston, Texas. Or go to St. Joseph's Hospital in Wichita, Kansas, or New York Methodist Hospital in New York City. Chances are a Christian hospital heals people not far from you. I have visited missionary clinics, hospitals, nursing centers, and health care facilities in Africa; and more are being started every day! Now stop and think of the doctors, nurses, therapists, aides, and ambulance drivers who feel Christ has called them into a healing ministry. Add the thousands of pastors who daily stand by a hospital bedside and pray for a sick parishioner—Christ's work of healing continues in our midst.

Once, on a trip to the Holy Land, I visited with a cancer physician from Houston, Texas, a doctor who had practiced medicine for thirty years, an oncologist. I asked him if he thought prayer made any difference for sick people. He looked at me in amazement. "Are you kidding?" he said. "I have gone into a room to see a seriously ill cancer patient. I listened as family and friends laughed and sang, put their hands on the patient and prayed to Jesus. As I daily examined the patient, I was amazed; the patient was getting better! Then," he went on, "I go into another room, a cancer patient, not nearly so sick, is alone, looking out the window, saying bitter things, even cursing. No friends, no prayer, no faith. The sick patient is getting worse—soon to die. Don't tell me that prayer in Jesus' name doesn't make a difference! I've seen healings a thousand times!"

Our college, Southwestern College in Winfield, Kansas, annually sponsors a "Nothing But Nets" basketball game.

You give $10, which buys a malaria net for use in Africa. Then, the general church (UMCOR) matches the donation so that we save two or more lives. We cooperate with President Bill Clinton and Mr. Bill Gates—and in the past half dozen years, this consortium has reduced the number of deaths from this preventable disease.[1] I believe Jesus, the Great Physician, is pleased and urges us onward!

Teachings

Jesus, the Teacher, taught, explained, and used parables even as he traveled. He wanted everyone to know and understand God's word. But ignorance of his teachings today is monumental. A 2009 Barna study found: "By the time most Americans reach the age of 13 or 14, they think they pretty much know everything of value the Bible has to teach.... In a culture driven by the desire to receive value, more Bible teaching is generally not viewed as an exercise in providing such value."[2] Amos, the prophet warned that the people would thirst for God's word:

The days are surely coming, says the LORD God,
    when I will send hunger and thirst on the land;
neither a hunger for bread, nor a thirst for water,
    but of hearing the LORD's words.
They will wander from sea to sea, and from north to
      east;
    they will roam all around, seeking the LORD's word,
    but they won't find it.

> On that day the beautiful young women and the young
> men
> will faint with thirst. (Amos 8:11-12)

When I first read Amos's words, I thought it strange he would say that without the words of God, people would go "from north to east." Usually we say north to south or east to west. Then I looked at the map. You can start in the snows of Mount Hermon, the beginnings of the River Jordan, the agriculturally rich hills and valleys of Galilee—the north. Then you can turn dramatically and go east—into the desert! A traveler on foot would perish in the wastelands without sustaining, life-giving water—the water of the Word. Amos's warning to the people of Israel should keep us awake at night: Where God's words are unspoken, beautiful young women and strong young men will fall down and faint from thirst. You don't have to be a prophet today to see people falling down. Jesus' teaching ministry helped those who heard him reclaim the heart of God's law and God's purposes in our world. We are meant to hear and do God's word.

DISCIPLE Bible Study has drawn out strange stories of biblical ignorance. A young lawyer in Dallas, as he received his first-year DISCIPLE pin, took me aside and told me, "I was baptized as a baby but never went to church until I got married. My wife dragged me to DISCIPLE and put a Bible in my hands. The group leader began by saying, 'Well, let's start easy: Let's open up our Bible to the Book of Genesis.' My mind raced," he said. "I remembered my

Latin: *genari* means 'to give birth to'! Then I thought—the generator starts my car. I smiled," he said, "and figured that Genesis must be near the front of the Bible!"[3]

The teachings of Jesus are basic to understanding the walk of faith, the Christlike way. Jesus couldn't personally teach everybody, so he sent seventy-two of his followers out into nearby villages, telling them, "Whoever listens to you listens to me. Whoever rejects you rejects me. Whoever rejects me rejects the one who sent me" (Luke 10:16). They did so, staying in homes that would receive them. They told his parables, they taught about the "way," glorifying God. They came back "joyously" (Luke 10:17).

The Gospels offer several examples of Jesus' teaching along the way that would lead to Jerusalem. He tells the parable of the good Samaritan in response to a lawyer's inquiry about how to gain eternal life. The conversation yielded the commandments from Deuteronomy 6:5 and Leviticus 19:18: "You must love the Lord your God with all your heart, with all your being, with all your strength, and with all your mind, and love your neighbor as yourself" (Luke 10:27). Jesus' response to the question "Who is my neighbor?" turned the tables by indicating that *we* are the ones who must be neighbors and who must care for the needs of others.

Remember his marvelous teaching about the rich employer who paid a full day's wages even to workers he hired late in the afternoon (Matthew 20:1-16)!

Another of Jesus' teachings challenges materialistic living and greed. Society tells us to get more, spend more, have more—get rich. Jesus warned, "Watch out! Guard yourself against all kinds of greed. After all, one's life isn't determined by one's possessions, even when someone is very wealthy" (Luke 12:15). He told a parable about a rich farmer who had huge crops, built bigger and bigger barns, stored it up, and said to himself, "Take it easy! Eat, drink, and enjoy yourself. But God said to him, 'Fool, tonight you will die'" (Luke 12:19-20).

On the way, the Pharisees asked Jesus about divorce. In his response, he challenged existing legal principles related to divorce with a more egalitarian view that showed compassion for women. He taught that marriage is a permanent commitment. "Humans must not pull apart what God has put together" (Matthew 19:6). Those who debated with Jesus pointed to Moses' law that allowed a man to give his wife a certificate of divorce. Jesus pointed to God's original plan for the relationship between husband and wife (Genesis 1:27-30; 2:24) when he replied, "Moses allowed you to divorce your wives because your hearts are unyielding. But it wasn't that way from the beginning. I say to you that whoever divorces his wife, except for sexual unfaithfulness, and marries another woman commits adultery." The apostles decided, "Then it's better not to marry" (Matthew 19:8-10). But Jesus said that not everyone will marry—not every person becomes a husband or a wife. "Not everyone can accept this teaching, but only those who have received the ability to accept it" (verse 11). Peter was married. Paul was not.

The parables of the mustard seed and the yeast teach about the growth of God's kingdom (Luke 13:18-21). Jesus' stories about the lost sheep, the lost coin, and the man with two sons give vivid pictures of God's love (Luke 15). Again and again, his teachings call us to show compassion and care for others.

The final word of Jesus to the disciples and us was "go and make disciples" (Matthew 28:19). The church experts say that the best way to make disciples today is by forming small, intimate study-share groups. DISCIPLE Bible Study with lay leaders is one way. We need thousands of groups in many languages around the world and in your town. Just like the class meetings that John Wesley formed in England, we need them to extend Jesus' teachings to the people. Just as Jesus taught on his way to Jerusalem, we need to teach vigorously today.

Some people believe that being "saved" is a "big bang," emotional moment. Those spiritual experiences are good, often powerful. I've had them myself. For many they are "conversions"—starting points for a new life. But they are just that—launching pads for a special way of living. Jesus insisted, "Not everybody who says to me, 'Lord, Lord,' will get into the kingdom of heaven. Only those who do the will of my Father who is in heaven will enter" (Matthew 7:21). Again, he emphasized "the way," the lifestyle of the Christian walk. "I am the way, the truth, and the life," he said (John 14:6). When we say "yes" to Jesus, we live differently than the ways of the world; we travel the Jesus way. And he spent his final days telling us how.

Our Lord not only wants us to know his words, to live out his "way," but also to teach others. "Everybody who hears these words of mine and puts them into practice is like a wise builder who built a house on bedrock" (Matthew 7:24).

Feeding the People

Hunger was prevalent in Palestine. Remember the Hebrews ate miraculous "manna" during their forty years in the Sinai desert en route to the Promised Land. Even there, drought often ravaged the crops and the pastures. Men who lost their tiny farms were often borderline servants, sometimes slaves, working for occasional food. Widows and orphans were generally destitute. The Roman Empire levied huge taxes. Often, the wealthy garnisheed land from overdue payments: The rich became richer; the poor became poorer.

Jesus understood hunger. He grew up in a tiny village in Galilee—a town of a few hundred people, some with tiny plots of ground. When he was baptized, he spent forty days and nights in the wilderness, praying and fasting— and almost starved to death (Matthew 4:1-2).

During his ministry, on the way that would lead to Jerusalem, Jesus miraculously fed crowds of people (Matthew 14:13-21; 15:32-39; Mark 6:30-44; 8:1-10; Luke 9:10-17; John 6:1-13). An important line in the prayer he gave to Christians around the world deals with food. "Give us this day our daily bread" (Matthew 6:11, NRSV). Perhaps his most dramatic teaching was in the shadows of the Temple. "I was hungry and you gave me food to eat. I was thirsty and you gave me a drink" (Matthew 25:35). The story continued with the response of the righteous: "When did we see you hungry and feed you, or thirsty and give you a drink?" (verse 37). The response of the king continues to challenge us today: "I assure you that when you have done it for one of the least of these brothers and sisters of mine; you have done it for me" (verse 40).

I live in Kansas, the center of our country's bread-basket. We raise wheat and corn, cattle, and hogs. Yet even here in an agricultural state, some people in the cities sleep under bridges. Some out-of-work people miss many a meal. Even in our small towns, children need free school lunches or else they would not eat that day. Thank God for church food programs, Meals on Wheels, Helping Hands, and school lunches.

In my Grandpa and Grandma Wilke's day on the farm, they raised a garden with potatoes, turnips, tomatoes, green beans, onions, and carrots. Grandma put up canned vegetables for the winter, made applesauce and home-made jelly, even cured cabbage for sauerkraut. With chickens and eggs, cured ham, and cow's milk—they never had any money but they always had enough to eat. I watched Grandma take jars of home-canned vegetables to the town's food pantry for the poor.

In today's world, starvation is rampant. Because of wars, civil conflict, economic injustices, religious persecution, urban unemployment, storms, and crop failures, millions around the globe are hungry. Many people, including tiny children, are literally starving to death. I am excited about the Heifer Project based in Little Rock, Arkansas. Heifer assists starving people worldwide to raise their own food by giving them goats and sheep, llamas, heifers, chickens, and rabbits. I will never forget when Bishop Machado of Mozambique came to me when I was bishop in Arkansas. Along with the Roman Catholic bishop, Machado had helped engineer a peace treaty in Mozambique after sixteen years of civil war. Now he wanted to raise a million dollars from Heifer, U.S. Aid, Rockefeller Foundation, and other sources to provide goats for the destitute! When he came to me, he needed $50,000 to complete the million. The Arkansas United Methodist churches responded—the goat project was put in place.

Heifer then launched their strategic plan. They gave one goat, usually a female goat, to a destitute family. A daily supply of milk saved the children's lives. When the goats were bred, a kid was given to a neighbor. Heifer veterinarians traveled the territory, helping nurture the food explosion. According to Bishop Machado, thousands of families were saved; they got on their feet again with their tiny farm plots. They helped their neighbors, all because Jesus fed the hungry and told his followers to do the same. I was so inspired by the Mozambique effort that I now give Heifer goats, sheep, heifers, and chickens at Christmas time in honor of my family members. If you wish to help, write Heifer at 1 World Avenue, Little Rock, Arkansas 72202, or call 1-855-948-6437.

I'm proud of our small town. Several churches offer one meal a week—different churches, different times—all with lay volunteers. It's Tuesday evening at our church. Then we have, as do most towns and cities, Helping Hand, the Food Pantry, Salvation Army, and some free meals in the schools.

On the Way

You and I are "on the way." Some are busy with work and family. While we are "traveling" through our lives, we have time to give used clothes to the Salvation Army, give money to a food bank or to Church World Service. Some friends of mine enticed me to join them in leading a DISCIPLE Bible Study in our local prison. I'll never be the same. I saw broken lives changed into Christ-centered lives. I keep up with some of them. One is studying in seminary.

In Jerusalem, in his final hours, Jesus spoke about judgment, about "last times." The Judge (Jesus) will separate the sheep from the goats (the good from the bad). These words are among his final teachings:

"I was hungry and you gave me food to eat. I was thirsty and you gave me a drink. I was a stranger and you welcomed me. I was naked and you gave me clothes to wear. I was sick and you took care of me. I was in prison and you visited me" (Matthew 25:35-36).

So as Jesus traveled, he was focused, headed toward his death; yet he took time along the way to heal the sick, teach the ways of God to those who listened, and feed the hungry. And as we travel, our Lord expects the same from us.

Questions for Reflection and Discussion

1. Review the Scripture passages discussed in "Healings." Which one appeals most to you? Why? What does it say to you about Jesus?

2. Read Luke 10:25-37. What does this story say to you about Jesus' ministry? What does it say to you about the way to live life "on the road" of faith?

3. As you live "on the road" of faith, do you spot busy people who are making a difference in the lives of those who are hungry, poor, sick, or in prison? How do they inspire or challenge you?

4. What could you do this week to provide food, clothing, care for the lonely and the sick, or concern and guidance for inmates?

5. What small-group experiences have been especially meaningful for you in learning about the way of Christ? What study experiences would you like to see in your local church?

Prayer

Dear Lord, we lead busy lives, working, playing, and traveling on the road of faith with Jesus. Help us take a few moments to feed hungry children, lead a weekly prayer study group, or call on a sick friend. Keep our eyes open, dear Lord, to daily ways we can serve and witness. Amen.

Focus for the Week

This week, consider what it means or what it might mean to you to live on the road of life as a follower of Jesus Christ. Identify one specific way you can practice love of God and neighbor during the week. Consider what it might mean for you to "set your face" toward this action.

1. For more information, see http://www.imaginenomalaria.org/ (accessed 9-5-13).

2. https://www.barna.org/barna-update/article/12-faithspirituality/ 325-barna-studies-the-research-offers-a-year-in-review-perspective (accessed 9-5-13).

3. Richard B. Wilke, *The Tie That Binds* (Nashville: Abingdon, 2008), 29-30.

Two Entrances

Scripture: Read Mark 11:1-11.

Jerusalem

How many people assemble for the Tournament of Roses Parade and Rose Bowl football game in Pasadena, California—three-quarter million? How many folks gather in New York City, shoulder to shoulder, on New Year's Eve to watch the ball drop—over a million? How about Mardi Gras in New Orleans? Or the Super Bowl? Jerusalem, in Jesus' day, was famous for its history, its location, and its ceremonial significance. Roman soldiers, the Jewish priests and political leaders, merchants of all descriptions, and a constant stream of tourists lived there. In addition, Jews all over the known world were required to go to Jerusalem to offer a sacrifice and celebrate Passover. Some lived in Israel and Judah, but because of the Assyrian invasion and Dispersion in 722 B.C. and the Babylonian exile in 586 B.C., many were scattered all around the Mediterranean. Sure, some people were sick or injured; some were destitute; some were slaves, but crowds of folks bumped shoulders during Passover in Jerusalem.

They called Jerusalem the "City of David" because King David made it his capital. His son, Solomon, built the first Temple. Partly destroyed by the Babylonians then rebuilt after the return from exile, it awaited King Herod to construct the huge masterpiece around the time Jesus was born. It was the talk of the known world!

Bethany was a village a couple of miles southeast of Jerusalem, and Jesus' friends, Mary, Martha, and Lazarus lived there. In John 11 we read that Jesus went to Bethany and raised Lazarus from the dead.

Palm Sunday

Christians remember and study Jesus' humble but dramatic entrance into the city of Jerusalem. He made it clearly prophetic, pathetically humble, and carefully designed to be a teaching moment. "Go into the village over there," he instructed two disciples. "You will find tied up there a colt that no one has ridden. Untie it and bring it here. If anyone says to you, 'Why are you untying it?' say, 'Its master needs it'" (Mark 11:2-3). Jesus was meticulously fulfilling the prophecy of Zechariah from centuries before.

Rejoice greatly, Daughter Zion.
Sing aloud, Daughter Jerusalem.
Look, your king will come to you.

He is righteous and victorious.

He is humble and riding on an ass,

on a colt, the offspring of a donkey. (Zechariah 9:9)

Surrounded by yelling peasants, disciples, folks waving palm branches, and people shouting, "Hosanna," Jesus wanted to emphasize peace, humility, and gentleness. The King was coming to the capital, not with sword and shield, but unarmed, and in love and weakness. He is a strange Lord, this son of a carpenter from Nazareth. During the recruitment of disciples, Nathanael said to Philip, "Can anything from Nazareth be good?" (John 1:46). Jesus rode on nature's most humble critter—a young unbroken donkey colt—his feet almost touching the ground. The crowd was cheering, shouting, "Hosanna! Blessings on the one who comes in the name of the Lord!" (Mark 11:9; see also Psalm 118:26).

Another Procession

But wait! We call it "Palm Sunday," but it was actually the first day of Passover. That meant that not only were hundreds of thousands of Hebrew people walking in, but much more dramatically, according to Marcus J. Borg and John Dominic Crossan in their book *The Last Week,* another huge procession also was entering the city![1]

The church, focused on Jesus, tends to overlook the secular side. Passover was a dangerous time—not only because hundreds of thousands of Jews gathered from all

over, but because they were under the Roman Empire—
Roman rule—and they hated the Romans. Many of the
Jews were "zealots," ready to take up arms at a moment's
notice to strike down the Roman authorities. Don't forget,
one of Jesus' disciples is referred to as Simon the zealot
(Luke 6:15; Acts 1:13). As a result of the Jewish revolt
against Rome in A.D. 66, the Romans ransacked Jerusalem
and totally destroyed Herod's magnificent Temple.

So, on the first day of Passover (Palm Sunday), Pilate
and a huge, showy military procession came into Jerusalem from Caesarea. The Romans came in force, to keep
the peace, maintain order, and to protect the Empire's
rule. In your mind's eye, envision the entrance of a vast
military force marching from the Roman seaport city of
Caesarea on the Mediterranean. Imagine Pilate riding in a
chariot, pulled by six or eight powerful stallions. Imagine
Roman officials in chariots or riding strong steeds. Roman
troops—troops by the thousands—would be following,
armed soldiers with spears held aloft, swords flashing, full
gold-encrusted armor glistening in the sunlight. It was an
occupation army of mighty magnitude. Residents would
observe the entrance in awe and bitterness. Passover
Jewish visitors might turn away and sneer or spit on the
ground, but they wouldn't dare shout out curses; a soldier
might cut off their head.[2]

So while a peasant preacher was riding in on a little
donkey, a procession of powerful imperial cavalry on
horses, foot soldiers with helmets, banners, golden eagles
mounted on poles, drums beating, was also marching

into the city. Not only observe the entrance as a contrast in political power, but look at the theological differences. The emperor (Caesar Augustus) was called "Son of God." His father, he claimed, was the god Apollo. Inscriptions refer to him as "son of God," "lord," and "savior." So Pilate and the political-military procession embodied not only a radically rival social order, but also a rival theology.[3] Jesus knew precisely what he was doing. He was ushering in a kingdom of peace—no more chariots, warhorses, or bows. Against the power, glory, and violence of the empire, Jesus was bringing a godly kingdom of righteousness, of forgiveness, of fair play, of kindness, and of peace. Zechariah had foretold what kind of king Jesus would be:

> He will cut off the chariot from Ephraim
> and the warhorse from Jerusalem.
> The bow used in battle will be cut off;
> he will speak peace to the nations. (Zechariah 9:10)

Confrontation

What did Jesus do after entering the capital? Keep in mind, Jerusalem was not just any city. On the first day, Jesus went to the Temple and simply looked around (Mark 11:11). Perhaps he remembered when he was twelve and upset his parents by staying behind and discussing Scripture with the priests (Luke 2:46-50). Now, since it was late, he walked to Bethany, and then returned the following morning. Immediately he confronted those who were buying and selling in the Temple. He tipped over the tables of the money changers and pushed aside those who were selling doves for sacrifice (Mark 11:15).

What's the problem? Integrity! The official money was Roman—coins with images of pagan deities and often, Caesar's face on them. But the priests insisted that those coins violated the commandment against graven images. They must be exchanged for Jewish coins before being given as a sacrificial offering. Vendors sold the animals that were used for the sacrifices, and doves were the traditional offering of poor people. Jesus threw the vendors out and quoted two prophets, Isaiah and Jeremiah:

"My house will be called a house of prayer for all nations [Isaiah 56:7]...But you've turned it into a hideout for crooks [Jeremiah 7:11]" (Mark 11:17).

Cheating is terrible, but it is especially bad when it's done in the church. We had a conference treasurer who for several years used church credit cards to pay personal bills. Only when apprehended, did he pay it all back to avoid going to prison. Some ushers have been known to slip twenty-dollar-bills out of the offering plates on the way to the altar. Some people have lied about their contributions on their income tax returns. Our God is the God of truth, of integrity.

Money is funny. Some people give regularly and sacrificially. A few church members tithe, but in my experience in the church, the average church member gives between 2 and 3 percent. Some givers get their names in print; others give generously, secretly—nobody but God knows the amount! One of the richest, most gracious ladies I ever knew didn't believe in pledging, so she gave her huge gift quietly a few weeks before the stewardship campaign—no one but the finance committee ever knew that she underwrote 10 percent of the church's budget! The funniest money story of my ministry happened when we sent key laymen, two by two, to every home to solicit pledges for the coming year. Two powerful businessmen called on a widow who had two teenage children. They expected a few pennies. Instead, she pledged a tithe of her insurance and social security income. The men objected, saying that was too much. (She made their pledges look small in comparison.) The lady, somewhat angrily, threw them out of her tiny house, saying that if she wanted to be faithful to the good Lord who loved her, if she wanted to obey the Bible and tithe that was her business, not theirs. She told them to get out!

Jesus confronted the ways of the world—lying, cheating, stealing, anger, violence, hatred, commercialism in the Temple—with the ways of God—integrity, compassion, gentleness, peace, and forgiveness. The Temple was to be a place of prayer, not a place for mercenary concerns.

Community

There was another problem with the Temple. It was separated into various sections or courts for Gentiles, women, Jews (men), and a Holy of Holies for the high priest. The holiest part of Hebrew Scriptures (the Pentateuch or Torah, the first five books of the Bible) declares restrictions on worship in the LORD's assembly: "No man whose testicles are crushed or whose penis is cut off can belong to the LORD's assembly. No illegitimate children can belong to the LORD's assembly....Ammonites and Moabites can't belong to the LORD's assembly...because they didn't help you with food or water on your journey out of Egypt" (Deuteronomy 23:1-4). Jesus was in the tradition of the prophets who called for justice and mercy and care for the poor over and above "right" ways of worship. Amos wrote:

> I hate, I reject your festivals;
> I don't enjoy your joyous assemblies.
> If you bring me your entirely burned offerings and
> gifts of food—
> I won't be pleased;
> I won't even look at your offerings of well-fed
> animals.
>
> Take away the noise of your songs;
> I won't listen to the melody of your harps.
> But let justice roll down like waters,
> and righteousness like an ever-flowing stream.
>
> (Amos 5:21-24)

The early church very quickly became inclusive. Do you remember the Ethiopian eunuch in the Book of Acts? He was a "God-fearer" who believed not in a multitude of fertility gods, but in the one great God of the universe. The

man was head of all the finances of his country. Why had
he been castrated as a baby? Probably so he could grow
up in the queen's court and never cause an inheritance
problem with an uncalled-for child. Notice in Deuteronomy
23:1 that he would have been prevented from entering
the Temple area. Read Acts and note that God sent Philip
to teach him about Jesus who was beaten and crucified.
When they saw an oasis, the eunuch asked, "What is to
prevent me from being baptized?" (NRSV). All his life he
had been "prevented"—prevented from having a family,
prevented from Temple worship. But now the love of
Jesus takes over. Philip baptizes him into the Christian
community (Acts 8:26-40).

Does your church have "handicapped accessible"
entrances and elevators? Do you have a special ministry
for mentally and physically handicapped children, youth,
and adults? Are people with Down syndrome hugged and
welcomed into your fellowship? Do faithful laypersons go
and pick up the elderly and those who live with physical or
mental limitations so they can attend church?

Jesus confronted those who used religion for their own
profit, for their own edification. He called to accountabil-
ity those who interpreted religious law in ways that made
it difficult for ordinary people—laws about food or laws
regarding the Sabbath. Jesus criticized those who would
say long prayers and then cheat widows out of their homes
(Mark 12:38-40). He watched some rich people proudly
toss money into the Temple offering box then proudly
walk away. Then Jesus noticed a poor widow who prayer-

fully "put in two small copper coins worth a penny" (Mark 12:41-44). He commented that many rich people proudly gave their spare change, but the widow gave all she had. The world tends to compartmentalize, that is, me against them, "those folks," "they're not our kind." Jesus reaches out to include the other, especially the outcast or the isolated: Samaritans, the blind, the lame, the prostitute, even a Roman soldier. Jesus builds community!

Challenge

According to Mark's Gospel, Jesus spent most of his daylight hours in Jerusalem discussing, debating, and teaching the Pharisees and the Sadducees—sophisticated scholarly Jewish leaders who ran the Temple program and cooperated completely with the Roman authorities. Mark reports that some leaders and supporters of Herod tried to trap Jesus: "'Does the Law allow people to pay taxes to Caesar or not?' . . . Jesus recognized their deceit. . . . 'Bring me a coin. . . . Whose image and inscription is this?' 'Caesar's,' they replied. . . . 'Give to Caesar what belongs to Caesar and to God what belongs to God'" (Mark 12:13-17).

The Sadducees did not believe in resurrection. They argued that if a woman had seven husbands, each of whom died, it would be a mess in heaven if there was resurrection. Jesus was clear. People in heaven will be like angels. Remember, he said, quoting their Scriptures, "God said to Moses, I am the God of Abraham, the God of Isaac, and the God of Jacob. He isn't the God of the dead but of

the living. You are seriously mistaken" (Mark 12:26-27).
Jesus threw the Scriptures right in their faces.

Soon Judas would go to these Sadducees and Pharisees to set the stage for his betrayal kiss. Jesus had confronted legalism, deceit, pompous pride, and religious
arrogance; and then he left the city.

What is it about religious leaders that tempts us to
try to be showy, to want to be honored, to sit at the head
table? Sometimes laypersons promote this behavior by
insisting the pastor or priest be constantly honored. What
is your evaluation? How can religious leaders be a part of
the fellowship and not constantly set apart?

Confrontation Today—the Jesus Way

Evil still flourishes today in high places and low. In
our world, social structures debilitate the poor. Political
entities, our government and others, sometimes use war to
try to solve political disputes. Daily we hear on television
or read in our newspapers of some business leaders
lining their pockets with money stolen secretly from
working people. Even church leaders sometimes exercise
political power to highlight their positions or strengthen
their authority. So, what should the Jesus people do to
challenge authority when it is in the wrong? Just as Jesus
without spear or sword challenged the Temple leaders, the
money changers, and indirectly the Roman authorities,
what must we do lovingly but forcefully?

I remember times when we Christians have stepped forward. I recall, near the end of the Vietnam War, when we marched down the streets in opposition to U.S. bombings in Cambodia. I remember vividly when our church joined others to march against an informal but powerful housing covenant that refused African American residents in a well-to-do part of the city. Here's a sidelight on that story. A key layman, Mike, a prestigious certified public accountant, said to me, "Sorry pastor, I'm not a marcher." "That's up to you," I said. A few months later, after our protest walk (which was successful), he invited me to his downtown office. He said he had someone he wanted me to meet. So I went. He took me into a side office and introduced me to a studious-looking young black man. We shook hands. Mike said, "He is a student at the university—an intern with us. He'll be the first African American CPA in the state." I went home glowing. Jesus was at work.

I tell folks I'm not a "Bible man"—I'm a "Jesus man." Look at the estranged, outcast people our Lord reached out to: the Samaritan woman who had been married five times, the Roman officer with a dying son, the demoniac screaming in a Gentile cemetery.

Worldwide, western powers are in tension with Muslims. Just as there are all sorts of Christians, there are all sorts of Muslims—peaceful, cooperative people on one hand, and hard-shelled, angry militants on the other. What should we Christians do? Of course, in our violent "armed nation" world, governments must be strong enough to resist attack. However, we must encourage negotiations and avoid unprovoked and unnecessary attacks. Further, as we practice the way of Jesus, we can encounter Muslims with kindness and mercy. We can remember the words in Exodus, "When you happen to come upon your enemy's ox or donkey that has wandered off, you should bring it back to them" (Exodus 23:4). Jesus put it forcefully: "I was hungry and you gave me food to eat. I was thirsty and you gave me a drink. I was a stranger and you welcomed me. I was naked and you gave me clothes to wear. I was sick and you took care of me. I was in prison and you visited me" (Matthew 25:35-36).

Questions for Reflection and Discussion

1. Read Mark 11:1-11. What challenges you or inspires you about this description of Jesus' entry into Jerusalem?

2. How do you respond to the views of Borg and Crossan that Jesus' entry was a challenge to the showy procession of Pilate and the Roman soldiers on the first day of Passover? What does this point of view say to you about Jesus' understanding of a king?

3. What do you think Jesus would say in opposition to various political or secular authorities today?

4. What do you think Jesus would say about various religious expressions in our day?

5. How do Jesus' challenges speak to you about ways to practice inclusive and accepting love toward others who may be very different from you?

6. What do you think are the places or times when we should gracefully and peacefully but forcefully challenge or confront powers and politics in today's world?

Prayer

Dear Lord, help us to be rooted and grounded in your love so that we will resist needing pomp and prestige. Help us to be so honest that we will be known for our integrity. Help us to stand for justice, integrity, and peace for all people. Amen.

Focus for the Week

This week, pay close attention to the news in our nation and in our world. Consider ways you think Jesus might confront and challenge various situations. Identify a way that you might confront injustice or evil with the way of Jesus. Pray daily for God's justice and mercy for all.

1. Marcus J. Borg and John Dominic Crossan, *The Last Week: What the Gospels Really Teach About Jesus's Final Days in Jerusalem* (San Francisco, HarperOne, 2007), 2-3.

2. Ibid., 3.

3. Ibid.

The Last Supper

*Scripture: Read Mark 14:10-26;
John 13:1-34.*

Jesus' ministry now moves toward its climax. Jesus had been anointed for burial by a woman, a believer. He had already been betrayed to Temple authorities by Judas. During Passover, the Hebrew people celebrate the Passover meal, remembering that night in Egypt when their slave ancestors sprinkled blood on their doorposts so that the angel of death would "pass over" them. They remembered that they would eat heartily, drink wine, and thus be ready for the full day of fasting on Friday, remembering when Egyptian oldest children, even Pharaoh's son, were dying. Passover dinner was ceremonially significant. They would eat unleavened bread remembering the no-yeast bread the Hebrews ate. It is no surprise that the disciples asked Jesus, "Where do you want us to prepare for you to eat the Passover meal?" (Mark 14:12). Christians call this day Maundy Thursday. *Maundy* derives from the Latin word *mandatum*—

meaning "commandment." Jesus gave a "mandate" to his followers in John 13:34: "I give you a new command-ment: Love each other. Just as I have loved you, so you also must love one another." We often refer to the meal as "Eucharist," "Holy Communion," "The Lord's Supper," or "The Last Supper." For Jesus, it was his last meal with the apostles, his last meal before the terrible Friday.

The Last Supper

Some of my cousins belong to the Church of the Brethren. I knew that "the Brethren" practiced a "foot washing" at their Holy Week Communion Service. My wife, Julia, and I were preparing DISCIPLE IV, and we wanted to include a "foot washing" in the final session, so I asked Julia to go with my cousins to see how the Brethren Church did it. She did. But just before the foot washing, just prior to Communion, the pastor made an amazing statement. He said, "This is a 'Last Supper.' For Jesus, it was his last meal with his friends, the disciples. So for us, it could be our last supper, that is, the last time all of us will be together, in the same place, for a meal with one another." That Brethren pastor made quite a point. Some of us will get sick, some of us will die, many of us will travel, a few will move away. All of us will never be all together for a meal again. It is often our "last supper."

Julia never forgot; now, when we have a big family gathering or church supper, she recalls those words. One last supper all together! Jesus knew he would not have the meal with them again until he would drink the cup "in a new way in God's kingdom" (Mark 14:25). Within hours Judas would betray him; Peter would deny him; the disciples would scatter; Jesus would be in chains! It was their "last supper." Have you ever sensed, as you ate a family meal, a friendship meal, or a church dinner—that it might be your "last supper" all together?

The dinner, for Jesus, was also "the Passover meal." Remember *passover* meant a remembrance by the Hebrews of their escape from slavery in Egypt. They remembered when Moses was a refugee herdsman in the Sinai—called by God to go back and plead with Pharaoh. They recalled that Moses used various tricks, magical signs, and wonders to persuade Pharaoh, but they all failed. Finally Moses announced that God was sending a plague on Egypt—the death of all firstborn children—even Pharaoh's. But the Hebrew families were told to kill a lamb and put the blood on the doorposts of their shacks. That blood caused the "angel of death" to "pass over" their homes, hence the name for the annual gathering in Jerusalem (Exodus 12–13).

Thus the Hebrews by religious law and tradition went to Jerusalem and to the Temple annually to allow the high priest to kill a lamb on the altar and to remember their deliverance from slavery in Egypt. They would celebrate Passover—their great memory of deliverance and liberty. Marcus J. Borg and John Dominic Crossman, in *The Last Week,* point to the differences between John and the other three Gospels, and they remind us that normally, for the worshiping Jews, the Passover meal was on Friday night. John's Gospel places the meal on the night before Passover, and the Christian celebration derives from this account.[1]

Mark's Gospel reports that Jesus, knowing dire trouble lay ahead, told the disciples where to go to find a room ready for them. They obeyed his directions to the letter, followed the man carrying water on his head and found the "upper room" fully prepared (Mark 14:13-16). Several important things took place in that "upper room" that, even today, continue to instruct, impact, and inspire Christians around the world. Jesus was aware that Judas would sell him out, that Peter would publicly deny him, and that the disciples would scatter like scared chickens.

Today some folks are baptized, confirmed, and then never go back to church. Many of us have opportunities to witness, to speak up for Jesus, and yet we often turn away in silence like a sleepy old dog going to his pillow. Will you, will I, have some opportunity to speak a word of witness for Jesus today?

Peter

Consider the "foot washing" in John's Gospel. Why did Jesus do it? What was he trying to teach? As they sat at the table, I'll bet everyone was talking—memories recalled of healings on the way, fears, angry religious leaders, affection expressed for one another. Jesus put a towel around his waist, picked up a water basin, got down on his hands and knees, took off the disciples' sandals, and began to wash their dirty feet. In our modern day, it is difficult for us to comprehend the dramatic symbolism. In New Testament times, only soldiers and rich people had boots—everyone else wore sandals. Paved roads were practically nonexistent—only dusty paths and trails. Few folks had chariots or horses—everybody walked—mostly miles and miles and miles every day. Filthy, dirty, dusty, and tired feet!

In our day, a host or hostess for a dinner party might greet guests with a "let me hang up your coat and hat." But nothing compares with the foot washing welcome of biblical times. In those days the youngest daughter or son might stand ready. A step of wealth higher, a paid servant—the same one who cleaned the latrines or did the dishes—would wash feet upon arrival. But in a wealthy home, the lowest slave would greet guests at the doorway, perhaps on hands and knees, and prepare to put cold water and dry towels on weary, dusty, dirty feet! What was Jesus' point?

Do you remember when James and John's mother bowed down before Jesus and begged, "Say that these two sons of mine will sit, one on your right hand and one on your left, in your kingdom" (Matthew 20:21)? Angry, the other disciples began to fuss. Jesus rebuked them all by saying, "Whoever wants to be great among you will be your servant" (Matthew 20:26). On another occasion, Jesus made his point by taking a little child in his arms and teaching that "those who humble themselves like this little child will be the greatest in the kingdom of heaven" (Matthew 18:4).

Now, our Lord took the form of a servant. He even washed Judas's feet—knowing full well that Judas would betray him before the night was over. But Peter was shocked. The big fisherman had seen Jesus heal the sick, feed the multitude, even raise the dead. For Peter, Jesus was Lord! "Lord, are you going to wash my feet?" he exclaimed. Jesus answered, "You don't understand what I'm doing now, but you will understand later" (John 13:6-7). Jesus was making the point dramatically: disciples are called to be servants, not big shots!

Jesus tried to illustrate his message. He rose up from the table, took off his robes, picked up a towel, poured water into a basin, and began to wash their feet. Peter still, like an obstinate school boy, doesn't get it. "No!" Peter said. "You will never wash my feet!" "Unless I wash you," Jesus said, "you won't have a place with me." Peter, typically jumping too high, too fast, shouts, "Lord, not only my feet but also my hands and my head!" (John 13:8-9). Jesus must have smiled when he replied that only Peter's feet needed washing.

Judas

Jesus knew that his disciple, Judas—one of the carefully chosen Twelve—had already made arrangements to go to the authorities. In the upper room at the Last Supper, Jesus said to the disciples, "One of you will betray me" (Mark 14:18). The Twelve couldn't believe him—they had followed him carefully and thoughtfully throughout his ministry. They had watched him do marvelous healings—even a day or two before—even the miraculous resurrection of Lazarus. They had listened to his teachings about the kingdom of God. They ate the bread when Jesus multiplied the loaves and fish and fed thousands of hungry people. Like Peter and Andrew, they all had left their day labor to follow him. "Betray him?" In puzzlement, they looked at one another, perplexed, asking, "It's not me, is it?" (Mark 14:19).

Jesus not only washed Judas's feet along with the others, he gave him the broken bread and the wine. John's Gospel tells us that he told Judas, "What you are about to do, do quickly" (John 13:27). Notice that God does not violate our self-deciding capacity, even if we cause trouble for ourselves or even if we self-destruct. Judas did both. He left the room and made his way to talk to the chief priests and the political authorities.

Why did Judas do it? Some people say he was a selfish betrayer—maybe out to line his own pockets, maybe trying to gain prestige with the chief priests. After all, he did go to them, sell out, take thirty pieces of silver, and, as we colloquially say, join "in cahoots" with some of the leaders—the chief priests. But after Jesus' arrest, Judas, in frustrated anger, threw the silver coins at the priests' feet. No, it was not self-interest. Perhaps Judas was tired of being bossed around, of being told what was right and wrong. Judas sometimes disagreed with Jesus. Remember, when Mary, Jesus' close friend in Bethany, poured extremely expensive perfume on Jesus' feet? Judas was upset and complained, "This perfume was worth a year's wages! Why wasn't it sold and the money given to the poor?" (John 12:1-5). Was Judas differing with his Lord's policies and procedures?

But Judas's suicide puts a different slant on things. If it wasn't the money, if it wasn't a policy difference, what caused the betrayal? Judas was a Jew. He was a loyal disciple, and in his heart he hated the Romans. All Jews hated the Romans; they had hated them for years. In A.D. 70, the Romans came down hard on a Jewish rebellion, killing thousands and totally destroying the magnificent Temple that Herod had built. The Jews prayed for freedom from the hated Roman Empire that ruled the Mediterranean world. Some Jewish men, called "zealots," prayed and planned for a violent overthrow. Now suppose Judas, who had witnessed the mighty supernatural power of Jesus, secretly wanted Jesus to overthrow the soldiers, the Jewish collaborators, and the mighty Roman Empire. Suppose he wanted a showdown between God's power and Caesar, who claimed to be God. Suppose a showdown would force Jesus to take up the sword, like King David, the warrior king. Gentle love, kindness, quiet forgiveness, healing, and sacrifice had gone on long enough. It was time for Jesus to take on the powerful ways of the world, and, as we say in Kansas, blow those terrible occupying troops clear out of the saddle. Suppose Judas was trying to force a showdown something like high noon at Dodge City!

Whatever his motives, and we really don't know them, Judas hurried to meet with the authorities. Later, just before the arrest, in the middle of the night, he kissed Jesus on the cheek to identify him in the darkness. But when Jesus gave love, when he told Peter to put away his sword and healed the soldier's ear that Peter had cut off, when Jesus quietly gave forgiveness and peace to all, I believe Judas had misgivings about his actions. Matthew's Gospel says, "When Judas, who betrayed Jesus, saw that Jesus was condemned to die, he felt deep regret. He returned the thirty pieces of silver to the chief priests and elders, and said, 'I did wrong because I betrayed an innocent man'" (27:3-4). He threw the silver down in the Temple then hanged himself (verse 5). Another account in Acts says that he used the money to buy a field, then threw himself down headfirst and died (Acts 1:18).

Holy Communion

In the upper room, when the disciples saw the bread, several thoughts must have raced through their minds. Perhaps they recalled when Jesus lifted up the loaves, broke them, and miraculously fed the thousands of hungry people beside the Sea of Galilee. Or as faithful Jews, they may have recalled when their ancestors were sustained by the daily "manna" in the wilderness as they traveled toward the Promised Land. The disciples would never understand the full meaning of the broken bread and the cup of wine until after the Crucifixion and the Resurrection. The disciples had not yet experienced the arrest, the trial, the brutal crucifixion—so they did not comprehend the full meaning of the words. They were like soldiers hearing a description of an oncoming battle, but they had not yet seen it, not yet fought it. The highlight, the eternal, God-filled moment—the action that has been reenacted around the world and across the centuries—is when Jesus took bread and blessed it, when he took wine and said it was his blood. Of course the full meaning of the action was not to be understood until the nails had pierced his hands and feet, the sword had ripped into his side pouring out his blood on the cross.

Across the centuries, almost all Christian communities celebrate some form of Holy Communion. It helps people experience God's forgiveness for sins and failures; God's provision of renewed peace, grace, and courage; and a fresh opportunity to surrender with gratitude to our Lord and Savior Jesus Christ and to renew our commitments to love and serve God and our neighbors.

Sometimes, in history, a difference of theological interpretation has caused denominational conflict, even angry splits and separation. The Roman Catholic Church holds fast to the doctrine of "transubstantiation," meaning that the bread and wine are "transposed," that is changed, into the actual body and blood of Jesus. Others hold to the doctrine of "consubstantiation," that is, the body and blood of Jesus coexist with the bread and wine, in the symbolic bread and wine. Many in the Eastern Orthodox Church and in the Church of England hold this viewpoint. Protestants often speak of the sacrament as a memorial or reenactment during which we recall, not only the bread and wine in the upper room but also the broken body and spilt blood on Golgotha's cross, Jesus' sacrifice for us and for our sins. While scholarly interpretations differ, Christians around the world and throughout history kneel humbly, remember when Jesus gave bread and wine to the Twelve, and invite his love into our hearts. Today, even though we still surround Holy Communion in mystery, we rejoice in the grace and peace we receive.

When I was fourteen, my dad, who had a funeral home, asked me to go to the railroad station to pick up dead soldiers, killed in the Battle of the Bulge in World War II. Some of the soldiers were fathers and older brothers of friends of mine. On Christmas Eve, our family was opening presents at Grandma's house, eating, talking, and laughing. My grandpa and grandma were singing *"Stille Nacht"* (Grandpa came from Germany). I was depressed. Our church did not have a Christmas Eve Holy Communion service, but I had heard that the tiny Episcopal church a block away did have one. I decided to go and asked the family to go with me; but they were laughing, singing, and talking and told me to "go ahead." When I entered the little frame sanctuary, I was pleased to hear the organ playing softly, to see candles sparkling on the window sills. Oh my! A moment of peace in a troubled world. Suddenly, the priest stood up and read the Scripture—the slaughter of the boy babies in Bethlehem by the evil Herod. "Oh no!" I almost shouted—"not on Christmas Eve." I was so angry I almost got up and left. But then, as the priest prepared the bread and the wine, he said, "It was precisely into our world of turmoil, of war, of evil, that Jesus came—and he came to save us." As I went forward, knelt, ate the piece of bread, and sipped from the Holy Cup, a wave of peace came over me. Jesus' body was broken for me; Jesus' blood was shed on the cross for my forgiveness, my salvation. I took a deep breath. The Holy Spirit moved through my body and my soul. I relaxed in Jesus' love, the Jesus who came into my kind of world. Thank you, Jesus!

The churches have cluttered Holy Communion with rules and church laws galore. My daughter-in-law, a local United Methodist pastor, can serve Holy Communion only in our local church, not in others. My son, a layman, cannot. In Disciple Bible Study, an ordained minister must come and give the sacrament to the study group. Roman Catholic women cannot perform the Mass; but in rural Kansas, a priest will consecrate the elements, and nuns will take it and administer it in their tiny rural churches.

I remember with joy my first appointment in a small rural church and offering my first Holy Communion as an ordained pastor. I recall the tears that came to my eyes as faithful members came forward, knelt, and prayerfully received the bread and cup, just as did Peter and the rest of the Twelve. The various rules and regulations of the churches are merely our feeble attempts to preserve the beauty, the sacredness, the holy meaning of Holy Communion. I did an outlandish thing once. On a church radio program, I consecrated the bread and cup, told my shut-ins to be listening, then sent laypersons to the homes with the consecrated elements. I didn't receive any criticism—nor any accolades either. But I didn't do Communion that way again.

One winter night, I was asked to take Holy Communion to a DISCIPLE group, a group of inmates at our local state prison. It was a bitter January night with frigid winds howling from the north. I parked my car in the designated parking area, half a block from the prison doors. I pushed my coat high on my neck, pulled my hat down over my ears, and half ran to the door. I'll never forget the awful clang of the metal prison doors crashing behind me. Just before offering Holy Communion, an inmate—a giant of a man, the size of a tackle on a professional football team—suddenly interrupted and said, "Why are you here?" I was shocked and subdued and silent. Then he softened a bit. "Why are you here on a bitter night when you could be home with your wife, by the fireside, watching television?" I hesitated, then with words that came from heaven, I said, "I love Jesus," then added, "and I love you guys." He mumbled, "No one in my whole life has ever said that they loved me." I now almost weep as I remember those words.

Holy Communion means different things to different people and at different times. Last Sunday, a young woman continued kneeling at the altar, tears of sadness flowing down her face. Was she in repentance, or in deep sorrow? Nearby, a husband and wife helped their young son and daughter take Communion. They were beaming with the joy of helping their children know Jesus. For some it is sorrow for sins; for some it is a steady faithful walk on the "Jesus way"; for some it is a plea for guidance from the Lord.

Questions for Reflection and Discussion

1. Read Mark 14:10-26 and John 13:1-34 again. How do these Scriptures speak to you about service? Are there any tasks of service you are challenged to do that are as humble, as servant-like, as washing the disciples' feet? Perhaps changing a diaper, scrubbing a dirty floor, or repairing an old house? What are they?

2. What thoughts or feelings do you have about Peter's reaction to Jesus washing his feet?

3. What do you think caused Judas to act the way he did? Has anyone ever betrayed <u>you</u>? How did it feel? Do you have loyalties today that you do not ever want to deny?

4. Can you recall a time you sinned and paid the consequences—a DWI accident; an adulterous divorce; a lie? Were you ever caught cheating in the classroom; given a speeding ticket; made a promise and then broke it? How was God present for you in that experience?

5. What do you feel or think about when you take Communion? Do you think of the upper room? Do you contemplate the broken body and the shed blood? Do you ask for mercy—for forgiveness? Do you pray for guidance in your discipleship walk?

Prayer

Dear Lord, I want to be a servant, like Jesus taught. Show me how. I do not want to betray our Lord as Judas did. Teach me the obedient way. Amen.

Focus for the Week

This week, reflect more deeply on ways you think God might be calling you to serve others. Make a commitment to one new act of Christian service that you can offer. Consider how your action might make a difference in the lives of other people.

1. Marcus J. Borg and John Dominic Crossan, *The Last Week: What the Gospels Really Teach About Jesus's Final Days in Jerusalem* (San Francisco, HarperOne, 2007), 110.

The Midnight Hour

Scripture: Read Matthew 26:36-46;
Luke 22:39-46.

Thursday night. Midnight. The Passover meal, the "last supper" with his twelve disciples is finished. Jesus had washed each one's feet to show the role of servant, which he emulated. Jesus had graciously given the bread and the wine, launching the celebration of Holy Communion for his followers across the centuries. He sent his betrayer, Judas, away to do what he was determined to do.

Midnight. Awful, "black" Friday is beginning; the sky is dark, pitch black. Our Lord knows that it is crisis time, time for serious, soul-wrenching prayer. He led the disciples once again across the Kidron Valley, onto the Mount of Olives, to the garden of Gethsemane where he took Peter, James, and John a little apart, and knelt down. Jesus threw himself on the ground and prayed.

A Man of Prayer

I shall never forget taking a group of church folks to the Holy Land and going into the garden. The garden, called Gethsemane, is a grove of olive trees. Some are old; some are ancient, having stood for hundreds of years. The garden looks directly onto the east wall of the Temple Mount and the Golden Gate. Nearby sits the Church of All Nations, built to commemorate Jesus' agony in the garden. As I and our little group knelt to pray, tears came to my eyes as I remembered Jesus' night of agony, of prayer, of final decision.

I believe that Jesus foresaw clearly the forthcoming events of Friday: the kiss of Judas, the arrest by the Temple authorities with the Roman soldiers, the trials before the high priest and Pilate, the beatings and lashings, even torturous death on the cross of Calvary. He knew exactly what lay ahead. He prayed so fervently, so intensely, that, according to Luke, his "sweat became like drops of blood" (Luke 22:44). He asked the Father: "If it's possible, take this cup of suffering away from me" (Matthew 26:39). Did you know that *gethsemane* means "the oil press"? Near where Jesus knelt to pray were the huge olive presses, used to squeeze the juice out of the ripe olives to make olive oil. Imagine the symbolism Jesus must have felt as his life blood was being squeezed out of him.

Jesus was a man of prayer. The church has often understated our Lord's lifelong prayer life. Truth is his days were saturated with prayer: prayers of gratitude, prayers for healing, prayers for his disciples. I believe that he knew the prayers of the Psalms by heart. On the cross, barely able to speak, he quoted Psalm 22, "My God, my God, why have you forsaken me?" (Matthew 27:46; Psalm 22:1, NRSV). In Luke's Gospel, when Jesus was near death, he cried out words from Psalm 31, "Father, into your hands I commend my spirit" (Luke 23:46; Psalm 31:5, NRSV). The disciples were so impressed by Jesus' prayer life—his ability to discuss matters with the Father—that in wonder and awe, they point-blank asked Jesus, "Lord, teach us to pray!" Jesus taught them and us to pray the prayer that begins: "Our Father in heaven, hallowed be your name" (Matthew 6:9-13, NRSV).

Jesus must have learned to pray and to listen to God as a child. His home was saturated with prayer and with listening to and obeying God. Mary, his mother, was visited by the angel Gabriel who announced the coming birth of Jesus. She listened and accepted what she understood to be God's will (Luke 1:26-38). Joseph listened to and obeyed an angel of the Lord who appeared to him in a dream telling him not to be afraid to take Mary as his wife (Matthew 1:18-24). Remember that, when Jesus was twelve, the family walked all the way from Nazareth to Jerusalem to celebrate the festival of Passover (Luke 2:41-50). His family was devoted to God. Jesus believed in and practiced the power of prayer. Once he said, "You could say to this mountain, 'Go from here to there,' and it will go" (Matthew 17:20).

Have you ever been in a prayer group, an intimate prayer fellowship? I will never forget one night in a DISCIPLE Bible Study fellowship when people prayerfully opened up, confessed grievous failures, and asked for insight for life-changing decisions. One lady was contemplating a divorce. She tearfully prayed for guidance: reconciliation or separation. When I was a tiny boy, my mother knelt down beside my bed and prayed. She prayed for me and for our family. She prayed expressions of gratitude for all our blessings. We had little money; her father had died suddenly; times were tough; I had a birth defect needing surgery. But she always expressed thanksgiving. Then she taught me to pray these simple words (I still pray every night): "Now I lay me down to sleep; I pray the Lord my soul to keep. If I should die before I wake, I pray the Lord my soul to take. Bless Mama and Daddy (I substitute other family members now that Mom and Dad are gone) and make me to be a good boy."

The Importance of Prayer

Several spiritual giants throughout Christian history attest to the importance of prayer. John Wesley said, "God's command to 'pray without ceasing' is founded on the necessity we have of his grace to preserve the life of God in the soul, which can no more subsist one moment without it, than the body can without air."[1] His mother, Susanna Wesley, raised each of her children with a time designated for each one of them every week. In a letter written to her son John, she talked about teaching them to read the Bible and to pray before breakfast. Martin Luther launched the Protestant Reformation when he nailed his Ninety-five Theses to the church door in Wittenberg, Germany. He believed deeply in the importance of prayer, and he asked his friends, often in a letter, to pray for him.

Mother Teresa, Catholic nun and missionary, devoted herself to caring for the sick and poor, and in 1979, was given the Nobel Peace Prize for her humanitarian work. Her life illustrates prayer as a way of understanding God's call. On a train trip from the Bengali lowlands to Darjeeling in the Himalayan foothills—a trip filled with hairpin turns and splendid views of the mountains—Teresa had a deep prayer experience. She heard the voice of Jesus; she conversed with him; and she had several visions of Christ on the cross. In prayer, Jesus and Teresa talked. Jesus told her to start a radically different religious order in India. Jesus said to her, "I want Indian nuns, Missionaries of Charity, who would be my fire of love among the poor, the sick, the dying, and the little children."[2] Thus began her ministry, recruiting hundreds of Indian nuns and ministering to untold numbers of poverty-stricken, sick, and dying Indian people.

These spiritual giants developed an intense personal prayer life built on the foundation of habitual and organized prayer time. Such discipline later exploded into a personal dialogue with the Lord that helped them form new methods of discipleship—the Protestant Reformation (Luther), the Wesleyan Revival with open-air preaching and class meetings (Wesley), and ministries to the poor in India (Mother Teresa).

Prayer as a Way of Life

Millions of us, in scores of languages around the world, use *The Upper Room* to help us launch our daily prayer. Devotional books such as this one are like ships leaving the docks and moving us out into an ocean of prayer, introspection, and thoughtfulness.

Sometimes we must pray for guidance, for courage, and for faithfulness as we face the future—knowing full well that danger, trouble, perhaps pain or dire difficulties lie ahead.

In my father's funeral home, we had an emergency ambulance. Those were the days before towns had emergency medical teams. One night, we had a blizzard, fierce winds, ice, and blowing snow. About midnight, we received a phone call from the police. A terrible accident—a car full of kids had crashed into an eighteen-wheeler six miles south of town. People were severely injured. We were to respond immediately! Dad and I scrambled into our clothes and jumped into the ambulance. Dad paused for a moment, said a prayer, and off we went. We knew we were in danger, but we had to go. No turning back! A veteran of the army told me that amid severe warfare he always prayed before charging into battle. He might be wounded, he might get killed, but he had to get out of the foxhole, climb the rise, and run forward, gun blazing.

Jesus and the disciples concluded Passover by singing a hymn, selected verses from Psalm 113 through Psalm 118. It is still a part of Jewish Passover Seder today, called *Hallel,* meaning praise—the root of our word *hallelujah.* Are the Psalms poems? Are they hymns or songs? Are they prayers? Are they Holy Scripture? I believe the answer is "yes!" Unfortunately, I have mostly read them as Scripture. Jesus, I believe, knew them by heart and selectively used them as deep prayers, often expressing his most profound feelings. As Adam Hamilton points out, "He taught from the psalms, he sang from the psalms at the Last Supper, and it was the psalms that he prayed as he hung on the cross."[3] Read Psalm 118 aloud and imagine Jesus singing it as he walked into the garden of Gethsemane.

Crisis Time

Sometimes it is "fish or cut bait." Sometimes no delay is possible, no turning aside. Have you been in a situation where everything is on the line—now or never—do or die? Jesus has traveled to Jerusalem. He has confronted the powerful Roman and Jewish authorities. He has overturned the tables of money changers. He denounced the noise, the taxation, and the showy celebrations of the priests, pleading that God's house should be a place of prayer. He knows that he has challenged the powerful leaders of society, and unless he flees, he will be arrested, ridiculed, beaten, and crucified. What to do? Take it up with God to make absolutely certain that he is on course, doing the right thing. If he is going to flee, turn aside, go back to Galilee, he must do it now. If he takes all his power and might and challenges the Roman Empire, he must do it now. If he stays the course for the next few hours, as the Savior of love, his fate is determined.

The Gospels recall his prayers seeking discernment, asking for clear guidance. In Chapter 1, we noted Jesus' momentous decision to go to Jerusalem, a decision made in prayer on a high Galilean mountain with Peter, James, and John. He knew precisely what that decision meant: challenging the power of Rome and Jerusalem. But now, in the final hour of crisis, prayer time is his alone in the garden.

I believe that Jesus in the garden was remembering his agonizing prayers for forty days in the wilderness (Matthew 4:1-11). During that time of fasting, prayer, and soul-searching when he was formulating his ministry, Satan tempted him. First "the tempter" suggested that Jesus turn stones into bread. In other words, you are starving, look after your personal needs. Now, facing death, should Jesus save himself? Then, "the devil" suggested he throw himself off the Temple towers to prove that he was the Son of God. Should Jesus do something showy and dramatic? Or should he continue the quiet, humble pathway of love? Last, the devil promised Jesus kingdoms if he would worship him. Should Jesus kneel down and worship Satan, yield to Roman and Hebrew authorities, or continue his pathway of total obedience to the Father? Jesus did not follow through with any of these temptations. Now, he was in earnest and intense prayer in Gethsemane. After this intensive prayer time, Jesus rose up from his knees fully obedient. He awakened Peter, James, and John and said, "Get up. Let's go. Look, here comes my betrayer" (Matthew 26:46).

None of us, of course, have ever had to pray like Jesus did in the garden of Gethsemane with sweat becoming as drops of blood. Still, we have had life-changing, life-determining decisions to make. One man told me he prayed half the night trying to decide whether to join the Marine Corps. It would mean leaving his wife and children, fighting in the war, and maybe being wounded or never coming home. A close friend asked me to pray with him. He was trying to decide whether to marry a woman who was divorced and had two small children. As a man who had never married, this marriage would mean immediate, heavy responsibilities. What should he do? Once, as pastor, a lady in the hospital asked me to pray with her. The doctors were considering a surgical procedure with a fifty-fifty chance of death. What should she decide?

I will never forget a family gathered in my study. A daughter in her mid-twenties would soon die if she did not receive a live donor's kidney. Tears came to my eyes as the mother offered, and the two grown sisters—both married with children—offered. Love and tears flowed. We prayed, desperately seeking guidance. When we said, "Amen," the older sister said, "I'm the one. God told me." They all nodded approval and left. I learned that the transplant had been successful. All were now healthy, and the family was filled with love.

Loneliness

Jesus was fully divine—the Word of God. But he was also fully human—the Word made flesh. He experienced every human feeling and life issue—including agonizing loneliness. Matthew's Gospel says "he began to feel sad and anxious" (Matthew 26:37). Clearly facing capture, torture, beatings, ridicule, trial, imprisonment, and crucifixion, he knelt in the garden to pray for guidance, for courage, for obedience. "He came and found them sleeping. He said to Peter, 'Simon, are you asleep? Couldn't you stay alert for one hour?'" (Mark 14:37).

If only his best friends would kneel by his side; if only he had someone like Peter to pray with him! Loneliness is a terrible thing. When we are sick, when we are suffering, when we are dying, we cherish a relative or friend who will sit beside our bed, hold our hand, and pray.

The loneliest experience I ever encountered was when I was helping my dad in the funeral home. A young couple had lost their baby—maybe stillborn, I can't remember. I drove the family car to the cemetery with Dad, the couple, and the tiny casket. We placed the baby in the grave. I returned to the car and sat alone and watched. Only Dad and the young couple stood beside the casket: no pastor, no family, no friends. Dad, a layman, read the Twenty-third Psalm. The couple stood in silence, and then they returned to the car—no words, no tears, no people—just a shattering feeling of loneliness.

Jesus, three times, pleaded with Peter to pray with him, to stay awake for a few moments while he knelt in agony. But it was midnight or one o'clock in the morning—Peter, James, and John were exhausted. They fell sound asleep, leaving our Lord to face his devastating future in awful loneliness. Of course, Jesus implored them to stay awake with him, to be in prayer, for another reason. Jesus would be facing trials, but so would they. Later, hiding out in some midnight gathering, three times when confronted, Peter denied ever knowing "the man" (Matthew 26:69-75). He needed to be in prayer with Jesus in the garden. The disciples fell asleep, leaving Jesus all alone to walk through the difficult hours of Friday morning.

Come pray with me, pleaded Jesus. Praying alone is powerful, but praying with others is more powerful still. One of the weaknesses of the church today is the decline in small-group prayer life. Jesus once said, "Where two or three are gathered in my name, I'm there with them" (Matthew 18:20). It is good to attend worship, but when a handful of believers gather in a home or in a fellowship corner, share their hopes and dreams, confess their agonies and disappointments, and plead for help in making a crucial decision, something powerful happens. The men and women, young and old, begin to pray with and for one another. Powerful experiences occur.

Sometimes when we are anxious, or undecided, or in turmoil, we don't "pray it through." Recently I implored members of our adult Sunday school class to share some of their deepest moments of prayer. One man told how years before he had been attracted to a young woman who was dating another fellow. He prayed until he relaxed, believing that God would decide. A year later, she broke up with her boyfriend, and they began dating. Now they have been married for nearly sixty years.

Across the room, a woman spoke slowly. Some years ago, she had cancer. Treatments were continued but were modest. At first she was anxious, then she prayed, "Thy will be done," and she relaxed—live or die she was in God's loving hands. Ten months later after she was well, the doctor said he had thought about telling her that she had only a 10 percent chance of recovery, but he decided against it. He told her that her peace of mind, her complete relaxation helped heal her body.

I remember when my mother lay dying in the hospital. Time after time, we thought we would lose her. Over and over we had prayed for her healing, but this time she seemed to know the end was near. She asked me to go find the old gospel hymn, "It Is Well with My Soul." I found it. We read it. We sang it together. She was totally relaxed; totally at peace. She simply went to sleep. She died in peace.

Jesus, knowing the awful suffering that lay before him, knowing the possibility that his disciples would deny him, betray him, and run in all directions, prayed for them. He prayed for clarity in his gentle, loving, but unrelenting ministry, "Father, if it's possible, take this cup of suffering away from me. However—not what I want but what you want" (Matthew 26:39). He prayed again, using the concept of "cup." "My Father, if it's not possible that this cup be taken away unless I drink it, then let it be what you want" (Matthew 26:42). In the accounts of the arrest of Jesus, we read about the kiss of Judas, the gentle reproof of a follower for cutting off the soldier's ear, and, in John's Gospel, the quiet manner in which he replied when asked if he were "Jesus the Nazarene." He simply said, "I Am" (John 18:5). He had "prayed it through." He was at peace. He had completely surrendered to the Father's will and purpose. He was ready for the cross.

Questions for Reflection and Discussion

1. Where are you in your prayer life? Do you pray daily? Do you receive help and guidance from the Scriptures and/or from a daily devotional like *The Upper Room*? What helps you? Does kneeling beside your bed? Does praying in the dark? Does praying first thing in the morning? Does having a prayer partner?

2. How does praying with others strengthen your prayer life? How might it help?

3. Have you ever faced a "crisis time" when you had to make a life-determining decision? Did prayer help? Do you feel that you made the right choice?

4. Have you ever been agonizingly lonely—praying by yourself—separated from everyone—desperately praying alone? What was it like? How was God with you in that experience?

5. How do you think prayer can strengthen you as you set your face toward the decisions in your life, even if they mean hardship?

Prayer

Dear Lord, in my life right now I want to do your will. I want to accept the responsibilities that are mine—even if that means hardships, sacrifice, and perhaps even suffering. Help me to be faithful, patient, even at peace in my soul—as Jesus was after praying in the garden; in his name. Amen.

Focus for the Week

This week, think about your practice of prayer. Consider your current prayer life and whether you might do something more or something different. What might you do to enrich your prayer practice? Do it daily and write about what you experience. Offer a daily prayer of gratitude for God's presence and power in your life and in the world.

1. "John Wesley on Prayer," http://new.gbgm-umc.org/umhistory /wesley/prayer/ (accessed 9-7-2013).

2. Richard Lacayo and David Van Biema, *Mother Teresa at 100: The Life and Works of a Modern Saint* (New York: Time Books, 2010), 24.

3. Adam Hamilton, *24 Hours That Changed the World* (Nashville: Abingdon, 2009), 32.

Taken Prisoner

Scripture: Read Matthew 25:31-46.

As a Christian and as a pastor, I knew well the teaching of Jesus: "I was hungry and you gave me food to eat. I was thirsty and you gave me a drink. I was a stranger and you welcomed me. I was naked and you gave me clothes to wear. I was sick and you took care of me. I was in prison and you visited me" (Matthew 25:35-36). Across the years, I paid some attention to all these phrases, except the reference to prison. I acted as if jails and penitentiaries did not exist; they were not a part of my ministry. We have a state prison a half mile from our home. In past years whenever I drove by, I would see a handful of inmates walking the exercise track; but they were not my problem.

Then one evening it happened. Two laymen in our congregation had received permission from the warden and from the chaplain to begin a DISCIPLE Bible Study for a handful of inmates. It was going well. They engaged in the study-share group for about two hours on Wednesday evening. Those two laymen looked me in the eye and said,

"Come join us." I mumbled something about being fairly busy. They responded, "Oh, come on. It'll do you good!"

So I did the necessary things. I took the prison training from the chaplain. I studied the rules, gave them my social security number and driver's license, and found out where to park. I did not carry a pocket knife. I learned not to be afraid when I heard the iron gates clang as they slammed shut behind me. I soon discovered that these men were human beings like we were. They studied their Bibles during the week and were ready to share, ask questions, and offer prayers as we met together. One inmate helped set up chairs around the table. About fourteen men—Anglo, African American, Hispanic, ages nineteen to fifty, plus the three of us—gathered. Our men's fellowship bought study books for each man and Bibles for those who needed one. I helped every Wednesday night for two years. I learned to love those guys. I prayed for them and watched their spiritual development. I even kept in touch with several after they got out of prison.

I'll never forget one night, a nineteen-year-old Hispanic Catholic inmate announced that he was getting out. He was being paroled that next Friday. I watched in amazement as he got down on his hands and knees. The others gathered round him and put their hands on his head. I awkwardly joined them. One by one they prayed that the Lord Jesus would be with him, guard him from evil, and help him make it on the outside. I was so emotional I couldn't speak or pray.

The inmates stopped being numbers or simply prison uniforms for me. One cold night, I spotted a guy wearing a nice warm red stocking cap. I said casually, "Nice hat. I'd like to have one like that." He grinned and said, "It's government issue. I can tell you how to get one!" I blushed. I didn't want to be arrested and go to prison just to get a red stocking cap! But the short visit was human, man to man.

The Arrest and Trial of Jesus

You will find the accounts of Jesus' arrest and trial in all four Gospels: Matthew 26:47–27:31; Mark 14:43–15:15; Luke 22:47–23:25; and John 18:1–19:16. Jesus knew quite well what was going to happen to him. He heard the rustle of the soldiers. He knew Judas was leading them. He woke up Peter, James, and John and said "Get up. Let's go. Look, here comes my betrayer" (Matthew 26:46; Mark 14:42). Prayers were over. Jesus was at peace—totally surrendered to the Father's will. Once again, he had set his face. Jesus was ready to offer gentleness in the face of cruelty, integrity in the face of corruption, forgiveness in the face of self-gratification, and love in the face of hatred. In other words, the Father's way, which Jesus was willing to follow, was the way of Calvary, the way of the cross. The Temple soldiers led by Judas were ready to take him prisoner. Jesus was ready to go.

Judas had promised to identify Jesus in that pitch black darkness. He gave the greeting by kissing him on the cheek. One of Jesus' followers (John's Gospel says it was Peter) grabbed his sword and slashed a servant's ear. Jesus said, "Stop! No more of this!" (Luke 22:47-51). Jesus healed the servant's ear. He was taken to the midnight hearings, to imprisonment, to early morning trials, and by mid-afternoon, to the cross. Those who were holding Jesus prisoner harassed him. They mocked him and laughed at him, slapped him, and whipped him (Luke 22:63-65). Jesus was a prisoner.

Jesus was taken to the Jewish Council or Sanhedrin where he was questioned. They demanded that Jesus tell them whether he was the Messiah, God's Son. Matthew and Mark tell us that the high priest tore his own clothes in anger when Jesus said, "You have said so. But I tell you, From now on you will see the Son of Man seated at the right hand of Power and coming on the clouds of heaven" (Matthew 26:64-65, NRSV; also see Mark 14:62-63, NRSV). They spit in his face and beat him.

Because the Jews did not have the legal power of life and death over a prisoner, Caiaphas sent Jesus to Pontius Pilate, the Roman governor. Pilate wanted no part of it. Jesus had not broken Roman law. Matthew's Gospel says that Pilate's wife had a dream that declared Jesus innocent (Matthew 27:19). Luke says that when Pilate learned Jesus was from Galilee, he sent him hurriedly to Herod who was in Jerusalem for Passover (Luke 23:6-7). Herod, you may remember, was tricked by his wife and daughter into executing John the Baptist, Jesus' cousin, by having John's head cut off and then presented at the birthday party on a platter (Matthew 14:1-12). After questioning

Jesus, Herod and his soldiers mocked Jesus, dressed him in elegant clothes, and sent him back to Pilate (Luke 23:8-11). Pilate had him whipped, said he finds no fault in the man, and appealed to the angry mob to release him. But the crowd insisted that Pilate release Barabbas, and inspired, perhaps paid, by the religious authorities, shouted, "Crucify him!" Pilate, in front of the crowd, did a highly visible "hand washing" and said, "I'm innocent of this man's blood" (Matthew 27:15-26; Mark 15:6-15; Luke 23:13-24; John 19:1-16). Then the soldiers stripped Jesus of his clothes, put a robe and a painful crown of thorns on him, put a stick in his hand (symbolizing a king's scepter), and led him away for crucifixion (Matthew 27:27-31; Mark 15:17-19; John 19:2).

Later, Christ's followers, inspired by our Lord's sacrifice, endured torture, imprisonment, and death. Stephen was stoned to death (Acts 6:8–8:1). Paul was often imprisoned. He mentioned imprisonment in several of his letters. To the Ephesians, for example, he wrote, "Therefore, as a prisoner for the Lord" (Ephesians 4:1). Again, to the Colossians he wrote, "Aristarchus, my fellow prisoner, says hello to you" (Colossians 4:10). Tradition says that Peter, often in jail, was finally crucified in Rome— crucified upside down, saying he was not worthy to be crucified like Jesus. Across the centuries, many faithful followers have quietly stood against evil regimes and have suffered imprisonment and death.

Have you read *Letters and Papers from Prison* by Dietrich Bonhoeffer? Bonhoeffer was a Lutheran pastor and theologian who was active in Germany in the resistance against Hitler and Nazism. He was imprisoned in 1943.[1] According to editor Eberhard Bethge's forward in Bonhoeffer's *Letters and Papers from Prison,* on Sunday, April 8, 1945, Bonhoeffer held a brief worship service, and then was summoned by two guards. As he left, his final words of witness were, "This is the end....For me the beginning of life." The next day he was hanged.[2] Like Peter, Paul, Stephen, and a countless host of others across the centuries, Bonhoeffer was willing to go to prison for his faith—willing to suffer—ready to die.

"I Was in Prison and You Came to Me"

The United States of America is crowded with prisoners. According to a report in *The New York Times* in 2008, our country has less than 5 percent of the world's population but almost a quarter of the world's prisoners.[3] We read about gruesome murders, ghastly mob violence, brutal rapes—that all happens. Many prisoners in our country are drug users, drug dealers, people who steal to get drugs. Drug trafficking across national boundaries is a huge problem. In some states, our prisons are overcrowded. Some places use "for-profit" prisons. I'm not an expert, but whenever I talk to prison officials, I say, "Most of the prisoners or former inmates I've encountered have (a) come from broken homes, (b) are addicted to drugs and alcohol, or (c) have learning or emotional disabilities." Many are black and Hispanic. The officials always nod their heads in agreement. I met an inmate in a maximum security prison who was a native of a Caribbean country. Armed men came to his house with guns. "Unless you swallow these drugs, catch a plane, go to New York, and vomit out the drugs to our dealer friends there, unless you do it now, we will shoot you, your wife, and your children." Somehow he was apprehended in New York and was serving time in Pennsylvania. Our society is pretty much asleep, but the church is waking up. First, we are remembering that Jesus was a prisoner. Then, we are remembering that he said, "I was sick and in prison and you didn't visit me" (Matthew 25:43). Those listening replied "Lord, when did we see you...sick or in prison and didn't do anything to help you?" Jesus responded, "I assure you that when you haven't done it for one of the least of these, you haven't done it for me" (Matthew 25:44-45).

Good things are happening in prison ministry today. A bishop, Gregory Palmer, in Iowa, established a congregation in a women's prison and appointed a full-time woman pastor. The church is now several years old, and the incarcerated women are attending services. Prison ministries are popping up all across the United States. In Kentucky, the Reverend Gale Wetzel, one-time conference evangelist, used to drive fifty to one-hundred miles each week to prisons. Mary Catherine McSpadden, wife of guitar maker Steve and daughter-in-law of the Reverend Byron McSpadden, for many years led a group of women in the Calico Rock Prison in Arkansas. In Georgia, the Reverend Diane Parish began a special summer camp for the children of inmates. In Alexandria, Louisiana, Joanne White started leading Disciple Bible Study in a prison where some inmates couldn't read or write. For several years, Bishop Ken Carder taught prison ministries to Duke Seminary students. Some of these students are considering a prison chaplaincy ministry.

If you say Pennsylvania, I think German, not Spanish. But the maximum-security federal prison near Pittsburgh is loaded with Hispanic inmates. It is called the Loretto Maximum Federal Correction Institute. Many inmates come from all over Mexico and Central America. At the request of Dorie Heckman, now deceased, and her preacher husband, David, I was asked to speak to inmates who had finished one of the Disciple studies. I shall never forget looking up at those gigantic prison walls topped with barbed wire and with armed guards keeping watch. Nor will I forget the stony stare of the female chaplain who slammed the iron doors behind me and studied my driver's license.

When I spoke words of congratulation and commendation to the Disciple students, I needed a translator because half the eighty men present were Hispanic and spoke no English. Later, since Disciple II, III, and IV were not available in Spanish, Dr. David Stains, fluent in Spanish, translated those studies. After all, some of those men were in for a long time—some for life.

It is hard, nearly impossible, for us middle-class Americans to understand the kind of poverty that would drive men into the drug traffic. Some are watching younger brothers and sisters starving. Some see their mothers weeping at night. I got two insights into the problem. First, as bishop in Arkansas, I recruited and sent a Hispanic preacher to Northwest Arkansas to start a new Spanish-speaking church. Why? Because massive chicken-packing plants offer jobs with low pay to Hispanics. A lot of Spanish-speaking people were moving in. We had no church building, so we used an existing "Anglo" facility. After a few months, I asked the pastor how his mission-ary work was going. "Growing," he replied. Then I asked, "Where do you find your people? How do you locate them?" "Two places," he answered, "at Wal-Mart trying to buy a pair of blue jeans and at the post office." "Post office?" I asked. "Yes. You see, some of the men sleep in their cars or stay six or eight in a one-room apartment so they can save money. Then they go to the post office to buy money orders to send money back to their fami-lies." *Wow,* I thought, *in that kind of world, no wonder a nineteen-year-old will wade across the Rio Grande at night, risking life and limb to carry drugs to wealthy, drug-hungry Americans.* I can't solve all the drug-related, massive, cruel economic problems of the world. But wher-ever we can, we can help men and women find the Lord, find Christian fellowship, and through integrity and hard work develop a sober and self-sustaining life. And we can also study our prison system to make it ever more just and appropriate.

Based on the "Walk to Emmaus"—a spiritual weekend for prayer and Holy Spirit experience—several denominations developed Kairos, an ecumenical revival experience focused on Jesus the Lord. An interesting thing happened in Kansas. Several of us met one night with prison officials. They said they wanted a spiritual retreat plan. We mentioned Kairos, but we said it would take some months to get the different denominations organized. They said, "We need it now!" Don Roberts, a friend of mine who farms nearby, spoke up and said we could build an informal spiritual program right away. We did. We call it "Brothers in Blue," and for several years, we have held Brothers in Blue spiritual revivals every six months in four different prisons. Each time, sixty to ninety inmates participate. Conversions occur, some inmates are baptized, enter into Bible-prayer groups, and attend prison worship service. Lives are changed!

The biggest life-changing event began in North Carolina. It is called DISCIPLE Bible Outreach Ministries (DBOM). Earlier, a religious group tried to enter the North Carolina prisons. They were a bit pompous, had their own program, and didn't want prison supervision. So North Carolina officials threw them out! Then two laymen, two Darrells, veterans of DISCIPLE Bible Study, went to prison officials and offered to take training, learn prison rules, and follow all prison procedures. They were accepted, began their weekly ministry, and enlisted other lay volunteers. Slowly, lives were being changed, and prison wardens and chaplains began to ask for this ministry. The last I knew, three hundred lay volunteers, both men and women, were leading those small DISCIPLE groups in seventy North

Carolina prisons. The organization (DBOM) headed up by Dr. Mark Hicks, now is reaching out into several nearby states and soon may become national in scope. Key principles are: (a) prison training, even veteran volunteers are required to take DISCIPLE and prison training every three years, (b) obedience to all prison rules, (c) faithful prayer and personal Christian discipleship, (d) support and encouragement by pastors and local churches, and (e) cooperation with Christians of all denominations. We are waking up, remembering that our Lord was arrested, and remembering that he said, "I was in prison and you visited me."

Aftercare

A Pew Center study cited in *USA Today*, in April 2011 says that four in ten offenders return to prison within three years.[4] We call it "recidivism." Why? They have no money, no jobs, no homes, no relatives, and no friends. Some of their addictions remain. They can get some modest friendship, some food, and shelter if they go back behind bars. And their souls have not been transformed. So, we must not only lead them to our Lord Jesus while they are behind bars, but we must also help them find productive lives when they are released. Relationships are essential.

A men's Sunday school class at First United Methodist Church in Wichita, Kansas, is an example. A work-release facility is only four blocks away. Laymen carefully negotiate with the officials. They can pick up prisoners at a certain time on Sunday, give them the church school and worship hours, and then return them exactly on time. During that experience, the inmates become friends and prayer partners with other men in the class. And class members begin to provide help for a prisoner. Does he have a driver's license? A man will help him. Does he have a skill, any training or education? A layman may put him in touch with an employer. Does he know about the special housing now provided for released inmates?

Three men I know, after about twenty years in and out of prison, were helped to find Christ through DISCIPLE. Then they were assisted in friendship by this men's class and are now making it "outside." One is a brilliant lawyer's aide, now clean. One is finishing seminary; he's nearly fifty years old, and then there is Marvin (not his real name).

Marvin gave his heart to Jesus in our study-prayer group and, helped by the men's class, got a construction job. But he hurt his back, lost his job, and then got in trouble by picking up a credit card on the floor in a casino. He tried to use it, but failed. When he was arrested, the men's class contacted an attorney who helped get Marvin probation for a year. He now serves the church as a greeter, has a modest job, a wife, and friends. I once asked Marvin if he had any family. He looked at me strangely and said, "I have a stepmother who knows my name." But now he has friends, men who take seriously the words of Jesus, "I was in prison and you visited me."

Questions for Reflection and Discussion

1. How do you respond to Bishop Wilke's description of his initiation into prison ministries? How does it inspire you? How does it challenge you?

2. What insights do you gain about Jesus from the overview of the Gospel accounts of his arrest and trial in the section "The Arrest and Trial of Jesus"? What feelings or thoughts do you have when you think about Jesus as a prisoner?

3. How do Stephen and Paul, both of whom became prisoners because they were followers of Jesus, inspire or challenge you? What do their witnesses in the Bible say to you about setting your face in a particular direction, even though it may lead to sacrifice?

4. Read a more complete biography of Dietrich Bonhoeffer such as http://www.dbonhoeffer.org/Biography .html or other resources. How does his witness affect you? What feelings or thoughts do you have about the way he set his face?

5. Read Matthew 25:31-39. What do Bishop Wilke's descriptions of various prison ministries say to you about the potential for such ministries in your community?

Prayer

Dear God, we remember how Jesus was taken prisoner, slapped, beaten, ridiculed, and condemned, then crucified for our sins and the sins of all—even convicts. Thank you. Help us to lead incarcerated women and men to salvation and to be helpmates. Amen.

Focus for the Week

This week, prayerfully consider ways you and your church might become involved in prison ministries. What is your church doing now? Do you have a jail or prison within an hour or so of your home? Could you talk to the chaplain to see what ministries are taking place? Could you and your church provide leadership? (For help, contact DBOM; Dr. Mark Hicks; mchicks@northstate.net; 336-454-5348.) Does your prison have a Kairos or Brothers in Blue spiritual weekend twice a year?

Contact Kairos at 800-298-2730 or check out their website at http://kpmifoundation.org.

Contact Emmaus at 563-585-2070 or check out their website at www.ecsministries.org.

Contact Brothers in Blue at www.brothersinbluereentry .org/. Do you have a "work-release" prison facility near you? Is it possible to make arrangements for certain inmates to be released for worship, church school, or men's or women's prayer fellowship? Aftercare is vital. Do you have church members, family, or friends in jail or prison? Can you see them? Can you write or call? Can you help their families? Can you help them when they get out on probation? A driver's license? A job? A place to live? For further study, an excellent book is *I Was in Prison: United Methodist Perspectives on Prison Ministry*, James M. Shopshire Sr., Mark C. Hicks, and Richmond Stoglin, editors (Nashville: United Methodist General Board of Higher Education and Ministry, 2008).

1. Dietrich Bonhoeffer Biography, Biography Online, http://www. biographyonline.net/spiritual/dietrich-bonhoeffer.html (accessed 9-7-13).

2. Dietrich Bonhoeffer, *Letters and Papers from Prison,* Eberhard Bethge, editor (Fontana Books, 1953), 11.

3. Adam Liptak, "U.S. prison population dwarfs that of other nations," *The New York Times,* April 23, 2008. http://www.nytimes. com/2008/04/23/world/americas/23iht-23prison.12253738. html?pagewanted=all&_r=0 (accessed 9-7-13).

4. Kevin Johnson, "Study: Prisons failing to deter repeat criminals in 41 states," *USA Today,* April 13, 2011, http://usatoday30.usatoday. com/news/nation/2011-04-12-Prison-recidivism-rates-hold-steady.htm (accessed 9-7-13).

Listen Closely— His Final Words

Scripture: Read Matthew 27:33-43; Mark 15:22-32; Luke 23:26-43; John 19:17-27.

"Father, Forgive Them"

Usually we pray for forgiveness for ourselves. I do. Each night I ask God to forgive me of any wrong words I have spoken or any bad deeds I have done that day. We pray in church, "forgive us our trespasses." Each time we receive Holy Communion, we ask for and receive cleansing, healing, and forgiveness. In Luke's Gospel, when Jesus is being crucified, he *offers* forgiveness to others.

Visualizing Roman executions is difficult for us—they were so unimaginably and intentionally brutal. Jesus was beaten so badly earlier that he could scarcely walk. The cross weighed about a hundred pounds. When Jesus stumbled, the soldiers made Simon, a man from Cyrene,

carry it the remaining yards to Calvary. The Roman
soldiers wanted to make crucifixions as ugly, as obscenely
grotesque as possible. Later, Emperor Nero crucified
Christian believers (they didn't believe Caesar was God)
by nailing them to crosses on the streets of Rome—
pouring oil and tar on them and setting them on fire at
night to light up the streets.

The soldiers were not content to drive nails. The
laughed; they spit in Jesus' face; they yelled, "If you really
are the king of the Jews, save yourself" (Luke 23:37; see
also Matthew 27:40-42; Mark 15:29-32). They stripped
him and they threw dice for his clothing (Matthew 27:35;
Mark 15:24; John 19:23-25).

Now it would have been gracious of Jesus simply to
have kept quiet. With his wounds, it was surely painful to
speak. But in the very midst of the soldiers' murderous
words and actions and to the leaders responsible for the
cruel decision, Jesus spoke softly to the Father, but loud
enough for nearby people to hear: "Father, forgive them,
for they don't know what they're doing" (Luke 23:34).
Powerful meaning screams at you and me. If Jesus could
forgive such beastly cruelty, surely he can and will forgive
you and me. Just think, no matter what you have ever said
or done, you can go to Jesus with a penitent heart, and he
will forgive you just as he forgave those who crucified him.

The other night, in our prison ministry, an inmate said
he did not believe God could ever forgive him for the
crimes he had committed and the people he had offended
and hurt. We recited this crucifixion Scripture, had him

kneel, gathered around him, laid hands on his head, and thanked Jesus for his love, his sacrifice, his compassion, and his forgiveness. The man said he felt a deep feeling of release, of freedom from the past—a sense of a new beginning.

I remember when a husband and wife came into my pastor's study and tearfully admitted that they both had been unfaithful, both had committed adultery. They wanted to forgive each other and start their marriage over, but they didn't know how. Only as we recognized that they had sinned against God, only as we claimed God's forgiveness, only then did they hug, kiss, and say to each other, "I forgive you, let's start all over again."

But wait. A second message is in Jesus' words: We not only receive forgiveness, but we are called upon to forgive others. Don't forget the Lord's Prayer, "Father, forgive us our trespasses <u>as we</u> forgive others." So, if you are one of Jesus' people, if you are a follower of the man on the cross who forgave even as his blood drained from his hands and feet, you and I must forgive.

"Today, in Paradise"

Wow! In Luke's account of Jesus and the bandits crucified beside him, one man rejected Jesus' love, and one man grasped hold of it. Both men were guilty as robbers, maybe murderers, maybe bloody rebels; both were receiving punishment. One criminal was bitter. He died with a curse on his lips. The other felt the forgiveness and responded to the love in Jesus' heart and lips. In fact he pleaded, "Remember me when you come into your kingdom." Jesus quickly replied, "I assure you that today you will be with me in paradise" (Luke 23:42-43).

Today! Some people teach that we lie in the grave until "Resurrection Day." But I believe in "Today"—I believe we can be with Jesus when we die. Here's why: Several years ago, I read about some "near death" and "after death" experiences—times when people had "died" on the operating table or in the hospital bed. The doctor had said "he's gone" or "she's left us." Then the person opened his or her eyes, blinked, and was alive again. Then came the amazing testimonies. People said they had seen a beautiful warm light, or had seen a dead mother or father, or even seen the face of Jesus. I preached on it in a sermon. Afterward, three or four people came to me—secretly—they had not told others for fear they would be laughed at. One man said he drowned in a farm lake. At first he saw only darkness, then all the bright lights of heaven. He was rescued and resuscitated. One woman said she died in surgery. She heard the doctor say, "We've lost her," then heard Jesus say, "Not yet, go back." So I believe in paradise, in heaven—Today!

My father was not an emotional man. That is, he didn't show much emotion. He was stoic, quiet, and businesslike. He owned and operated a funeral home. After a long time of a down economy, in the thirties, when people couldn't pay their funeral bills, Dad needed a new hearse. He thought and debated but couldn't decide. One night he prayed, asking God to help him decide. An amazing thing happened: His mother, who had been dead for a couple of years, came to him and said, "Buy the hearse, son." It never happened before; it never happened again—but Dad bought the hearse! He was never sorry. The hearse served many families with beauty and dignity for many years.

I don't know what happened to the murdering thief who cursed God and died. Some say "Hell"; some say "Sheol" (a place of nonexistent darkness); some say God will figure out a way to save them; some say everybody will go to heaven. I don't know everything God is doing. I do know that some people, like the unrepentant thief, live and die in bitterness and unrepentant hate—even curse God and die. But the thief who turned to Jesus in faith heard the words, "Today you will be with me in paradise."

"Here Is Your Son.... Here Is Your Mother"

John's Gospel tells us that three women stood with John, the beloved, at the foot of the cross. One was Mary of Magdala. The Scriptures say that Jesus cast out demons and thus healed her (Mark 16:9; Luke 8:2). When Jesus healed her of her terrible tremors, she became a devoted follower. Tradition says she was a prostitute. Remember, she was the first one Jesus appeared to at the empty tomb (Mark 16:9; John 20:11-18). She and Mary, the mother of James, and Salome were planning to apply customary spices to his dead body (Mark 16:1). The second woman at the Crucifixion was Mary, the wife of Clopas. This lady was Jesus' mother's sister by marriage. Joseph, Jesus' earthly father, had a brother, Clopas, and his wife was also named Mary. Scholars believe that Joseph died when Jesus was young. The last we hear of him in the Gospels is when Jesus was twelve. Clopas may have helped provide for Joseph's wife, Mary, and her children. The two Marys stood together at the cross, perhaps arm in arm. We learn from early church fathers that Clopas and Mary's son, Symeon, became leader of the church in Jerusalem after the deaths of James and Peter.[1] But Jesus, scarcely able to breathe, blood dripping from his hands and feet, looked down on his mother, Mary. As she stared at her dying son, memories must have raced through her mind: that humble birth in the stable in Bethlehem, that frightening flight into Egypt to avoid Herod's wrath, and that time in Jerusalem when Jesus was twelve and stayed behind, talking to the wise scholars.

Near death, Jesus also looked at "the disciple whom he loved" who was standing nearby (John 19:26). Jesus was not subtle. He said: "Woman, here is your son." Then he said to the disciple, "Here is your mother" (John 19:26-27). They became family. It is a wonderful thing when, after a death, a tragedy, families stick together, care for one another—sometimes caring for a distant relative or friend. But don't stop reading. The next words here are riveting: "And from that time on, this disciple took her into his home" (verse 27). The beloved disciple obeyed Jesus. He took care of Mary as long as she lived.

"Why Have You Left Me?"

They were laughing at him. The chief priests and top scribes mockingly called out, "He saved others . . . but he can't save himself" (Mark 15:31). Some shook their heads and shouted insults, "Ha! So you were going to destroy the temple and rebuild it in three days, were you? . . . come down from that cross!" (Mark 15:30). Jesus heard these jeers as he agonized in pain. Blood oozed from his hands and feet; he could scarcely breathe. He was minutes away from dying. Then he whispered these words: "'Eloi, Eloi, lama sabachthani' which means, 'My God, my God, why have you left me?'" (Mark 15:34).

I am first grabbed by the word "why." That word comes out of our mouths whenever the innocent suffer. When we see little children shot and killed in a Newtown, Connecticut, schoolhouse, we ask "why?" When a young lady, a Sunday school teacher and mother of two, has her neck slashed by a drunken house robber, we ask "why?" Students of the Bible know the story of Job. He was faithful to God in every way. He was a man of absolute integrity. He not only gave his tithe, but he over-gave regularly. Continually he noticed the poor, widows, and orphans and gave them food and shelter. His life was saturated in prayer. He raised his children to be God-fearing, faithful people. When Job's world fell apart—his children died, his wealth was taken away, his body was racked with pain—he asked "why?" Friends tried to be helpful, but their answers were irrelevant and untrue.

Apparently, to the "why?" question, we are left without an answer except, "someday we will understand." After further study, we see that Jesus was encountering the total human experience. He was not only suffering, not only dying, but he also was enveloping in his body and soul the lonely, human experience of feeling apart, separated from the Father.

But wait. That's not the whole story. Most folks don't realize that Jesus is quoting the twenty-second psalm. He learned the Psalms at his mother Mary's knee; perhaps walking to work with his father, Joseph. Now, as we read Psalm 22, we note that it begins with "why?" and continues with the feeling of isolation:

> My God! My God,
>   why have you left me all alone? (verse 1).
> All who see me make fun of me (verse 7).
> I can count all my bones! (verse 17).
> They divvy up my garments among themselves;
>   they cast lots for my clothes (verse 18).

But the psalm continues as a poem of actual experience and fantastic faith:

> But you, LORD! Don't be far away!
>   You are my strength! (verse 19).
> I offer praise in the great congregation because of you;
>   I will fulfill my promises (verse 25).

They will proclaim God's righteousness to those not
yet born,
   telling them what God has done (verse 31).

So this near-final word from the cross is a meditation of
a powerful psalm that expresses loneliness and sorrow, as
well as faith and final victory.

"I Am Thirsty"

Three times, according to the Gospels, the soldiers
offered Jesus wine. Mark's Gospel says, right before
the Crucifixion, "They tried to give him wine mixed with
myrrh" (Mark 15:23). Matthew uses the word "vinegar."
But notice, Jesus tasted the wine, and then refused to
drink it (Matthew 27:34). Jesus was intentionally choosing
to fully suffer for our sins and the sins of the whole world.
Jesus chose to identify with the suffering of all humankind.
He faced sin, evil, despair, and death head on!

Adam Hamilton, in *Final Words from the Cross,*
reminds us that in today's world we tend to choose the
easy way out. "If we feel bad, we want a pill. If things
aren't going well, we want a quick fix . . . we want to
minimize pain and to avoid the way that's uncomfortable
or inconvenient."[2] Hamilton tells us that his volunteer
work team that went to Mississippi following Hurricane
Katrina did not stay in hotels but rather slept on the floors
of churches or in tents. "Why? Because they wanted to
identify with the people . . . in their suffering."[3]

The second offer of wine took place after Jesus was nailed to the cross. Luke records that the soldiers offered wine in the midst of mockery, almost as if they were giving him a toast. "The soldiers also mocked him. They came up to him, offering him sour wine and saying, 'If you really are the king of the Jews, save yourself.' Above his head was a notice of the formal charge against him. It read 'This is the king of the Jews'" (Luke 23:36-38).

Jesus fulfilled his mission—to live, to love, and to die for the entire human race. Now the moment of death has come. Jesus was fulfilling the full human experience. John's Gospel tells us that Jesus said, "I am thirsty" (John 19:28). Soldiers responded. They soaked a sponge in sour wine and, with a hyssop branch, reached up and touched his lips. Jesus received the wine, then died. Often when people are dying, their lips are parched, their mouth dries up, and their tongue seems stiff. I have seen a nurse put a damp sponge on a dying woman's lips. Perhaps you have put a finger on the top of a straw, taken that straw half-filled with water, and let it drop into some person's mouth. Maybe you or a nurse's aide have taken a couple of broken ice cubes and gently separated the lips of a family member or friend and placed them in the dying, dry mouth. I have.

"It Is Finished"

Do you remember the last time you breathed a sigh of relief when you had finished an important job? Do you recall a moment when, perhaps with sweaty palms or with a tired, worn-out feeling, you exclaimed, "Done! It's finished!" Maybe you had just completed a term paper for English literature. Or maybe you had moved into a new home and you finally had all the furniture arranged. Maybe you attended the college graduation of your oldest son or daughter and you secretly breathed a sigh of relief and said to your spouse, "Whew! It's over. We did it!"

Of course nothing compares with the completion of Jesus' ministry in human flesh on earth. He has, as a human teacher-physician, given his last Sermon on the Mount, healed his last leper, quieted his last storm, and held the last child in his arms. He has faithfully followed the Father's plan for him to love those who hate, forgive those who sinned, and raise some, like Lazarus, from the dead.

John's Gospel tells us that Jesus uttered the words "It is finished" right before he died (John 19:30, NRSV). "Finished!" It is not the word of defeat; it is the word of victory—of completion. The Common English Bible uses this sense in its translation, "It is completed." Will Willimon claims these words of Jesus as something similar to what Michelangelo might have said while he was looking up at the Sistine Chapel after he had completed the last brushstroke of that long, arduous task: "It is finished!"[4]

Christians across the centuries have seen the cross as the culminating work of God for the salvation of humankind. We call it *atonement*—and it has been interpreted, in the Bible and in history, in many ways. In John's Gospel, Jesus' death is an atoning sacrifice to save us from sin.

It is also a sacrifice to save us from death. The cross is a demonstration of divine love for all humanity. It is a model we are to use for practicing sacrificial love. Some see it as a sign of God's ultimate triumph over death. Without doubt, Jesus in his death identifies with our human pain, our suffering and human mortality.[5] The apostle Paul summarizes the work of Jesus—his life, death, and resurrection, including the tragic but glorious cross—by saying simply, "I'm not ashamed of the gospel: it is God's own power for salvation to all who have faith in God" (Romans 1:16).

"Into Your Hands"

"Father, into your hands I entrust my life" (Luke 23:46). Luke's Gospel tells us that after he had said these words, Jesus breathed his last breath. It was over—over until the Resurrection, new life in Christ, new life for the disciples, for Mary, and for us.

I have known these words for my lifetime—but I did not know where they came from. Do you? Did you know, in addition to the horrendous impact of the historic moment of Jesus' death, Jesus is quoting from a psalm? We have argued earlier that Jesus was a man of prayer—that he learned the Psalms, perhaps at his mother's knee. The Psalms were, and are, the Hebrew hymnbook. I'll bet you know a lot of spiritual hymns and songs that are a part of the Protestant heritage. I do—songs like "The Old Rugged Cross," "Blest Be the Tie," "Blessed Assurance," and "Rescue the Perishing." The final words of Jesus are a

prayer and a direct quotation of Psalm 31:5. Here are the
first five verses:

I take refuge in you, LORD.
Please never let me be put to shame.
Rescue me by your righteousness!
Listen closely to me!
Deliver me quickly;
be a rock that protects me;
be a strong fortress that saves me!
You are definitely my rock and my fortress.
Guide me and lead me for the sake of your good name!
Get me out of this net that's been set for me
because you are my protective fortress.
I entrust my spirit into your hands;
you, LORD, God of faithfulness—
you have saved me.

(Psalm 31:1-5)

Please pick up a Bible and read the entire psalm. Written years before Jesus, it is so appropriate for Jesus' life,
his sufferings, his ministry, and his death in the Father's
love. No wonder that our Lord was meditating on it, perhaps whispering it to himself in his dying moments, quoting the surrender, committal verse as his last human
utterance. "Father, into your hands I entrust my life."

Death was not God's final word. God's word in Jesus
Christ is *life*. As our Lenten study draws to a close on
this Easter Day, it is appropriate that we end on the final

words of Jesus on the cross—the Savior who was a man of prayer; who set his face to Jerusalem; who taught and wishes us to teach; who healed and wishes us to heal; who fed the hungry and wishes us to remember the poor, the starving, and the naked; who went into jail as a prisoner and wants us to take the gospel of love and forgiveness—of life-changing redemption into the prisons. Now it is time to celebrate Easter, for the Jesus who died on the cross is the Lord Jesus who rose three days later and about whom the two men in the tomb asked the women, "Why do you look for the living among the dead?" (Luke 24:5).

Questions for Reflection and Discussion

1. Has anyone, long time past or recently, hurt, offended, or betrayed you? What does Jesus' forgiveness mean to you? How does it witness to your need to forgive or to be forgiven?

2. Read Luke 23:39-43 about the way the two criminals responded to Jesus. How do their responses speak to you? What do you imagine when you hear the word *paradise*?

3. Read John 19:26-27. What feelings or thoughts do you have about Jesus' concern for his mother as he suffered on the cross?

4. When have you felt lonely and abandoned by God? What was it like? How was God present for you in the midst of those feelings?

5. Do you agree with Adam Hamilton's observation that we generally want a quick fix or an easy way out of difficult times? (See the section "I Am Thirsty.") Reflect on your response. What experiences in your life might illustrate the need for an easy way out?

6. When have you had a sense of completion in your life? What was it like?

7. Read Psalm 31. How do you think deep commitment and trust in God gets us through rough times? What have your experiences been like?

8. How do these words of Jesus from the cross prepare you to celebrate Easter and the Resurrection?

Prayer

Dear Lord, in amazement we meditate on your love—your love so vividly demonstrated on Calvary's cross. Help us right now to surrender fully to that amazing grace and know we are accepted as your people. Amen.

Focus for the Week

This week, consider prayerfully how Jesus' willingness to "set his face" to Jerusalem, to his suffering, death, and resurrection, inspire or challenge you to "set your face" to new life and hope.

1. Adam Hamilton, *Final Words from the Cross* (Nashville: Abingdon, 2011), 53
2. Ibid., 88.
3. Ibid.
4. Ibid., 104.
5. Ibid., 106-108.

DISCIPLE

Search Scripture...Find Community
The #1 choice in long-term Bible studies for more than 20 years
To learn more visit Disciple.Cokesbury.com

check out other resources by
BISHOP RICHARD B. WILKE

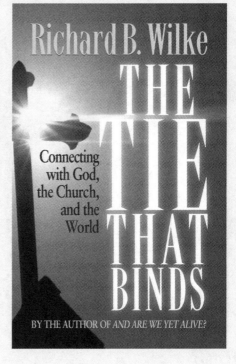

9780687660346   9780687652082

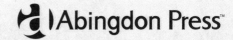

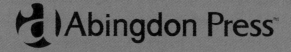